Break Free from Burnout
8 Areas of Wellness
You Need to Build Resilience

Steven M. Walters

First Edition
2025

Published by Educational Advising and Consulting, LLC

© 2025 Educational Advising and Consulting, LLC. All rights reserved.

ISBN: 979-8-9925579-0-9

Printed in USA

For more information, visit www.unfryd.com

Dedication

To everyone striving to build a resilient and fulfilling life—this book is for you.

To my family and friends, whose unwavering support and encouragement have been the foundation of my own resilience, thank you for inspiring me every day.

To the students, entrepreneurs, parents, employees, and professionals I've had the privilege to work with—you've shown me that resilience isn't just a concept; it's a way of life.

And finally, to you, the reader—may this book be the starting point of a journey that brings balance, strength, and clarity to every area of your wellness.

Table of Contents

Preface:
Laying the Foundation for Resilience

Congratulations on taking the first step toward redefining how you live, work, and thrive. In a world full of challenges and competing demands, resilience isn't just a luxury, it's a necessity. Life constantly presents obstacles, from managing daily responsibilities to navigating unexpected stress. But what if these challenges weren't barriers to avoid but stepping stones toward a stronger, more purposeful life?

Resilience is the key to thriving, not just surviving. It equips you with the clarity, confidence, and adaptability to face life's challenges with grace, turning stress into strength and setbacks into opportunities. By cultivating resilience, you'll discover how to transform chaos into balance and move through life with greater confidence and purpose.

This book is your companion for creating meaningful changes, offering practical guidance and actionable strategies tailored to your unique needs. Every chapter empowers you to take small, intentional steps toward cultivating resilience across eight interconnected areas of human wellness: Physical, Intellectual, Emotional, Financial, Occupational, Social, Spiritual, and Environmental. These areas are deeply connected, and progress in one can create a ripple effect, strengthening the others and fostering a balanced, fulfilling life.

Resilience isn't about perfection, it's about progress. Whether you're a student juggling coursework and personal growth, an entrepreneur navigating the complexities of running a business, or a parent managing the demands of a busy household, resilience empowers you to approach life's demands with grace and adaptability.

At the heart of this journey is the Wheel of Success, a framework developed through years of research, personal experience, and coaching. It focuses on six foundational pillars: Time Management, Goal Setting, Motivation, Success and Failure, Stress Management, and Self-Awareness. These pillars revolve around personal accountability, emphasizing that your actions drive meaningful change. Mastering these principles empowers you to avoid burnout and build a life rooted in balance, confidence, and purpose. Visit my website, Unfryd.com To Learn more about the Wheel of Success.

Pause for a moment and consider:
- *What's one area of your life where resilience could make the most transformative difference?*

- *How could building resilience in that area impact your overall well-being?*

Don't worry if you're not sure about how to answer these questions yet. The answers will come soon enough.

This book was written as a guide to create positive, lasting changes. As you journey through its pages, you'll uncover tools to transform stress into strength, achieve balance, and design a life of fulfillment and purpose.

Get ready to take the first intentional step toward reshaping your life. Your journey begins now.

Part 1
The Foundation of Resilience

The Power of Resilience: Why It Matters

In today's fast-paced and unpredictable world, resilience is more than a desirable trait—it's an essential skill. Every day, we face stressors that test our patience, adaptability, and strength, whether it's balancing demanding schedules, managing relationships, or navigating unexpected challenges. Resilience empowers us to endure, recover, and thrive. It transforms life's difficulties into opportunities for growth, equipping us to move forward with clarity and confidence.

At its core, resilience enables you to break free from the reactive cycle of stress and overwhelm. It becomes the foundation of emotional strength, mental clarity, and physical vitality, helping you transform setbacks into stepping stones and challenges into opportunities for growth. Imagine moving through life with clarity and control, embracing each challenge as a chance to grow stronger and more adaptable.

Resilience isn't a one-size-fits-all approach—it looks different for everyone. For a busy parent, it might mean managing competing priorities without feeling burned out. For a student, resilience could involve building the emotional and mental strength to overcome academic challenges. For someone navigating a career, it might focus on transforming workplace stress into motivation for meaningful growth. Whatever your circumstances, resilience empowers you to take control of your narrative, fostering a sense of purpose and direction.

Think of resilience as a powerful muscle that grows stronger with intentional practice. Like any skill, it requires consistent effort and the right tools to develop. This book provides those tools, guiding you step by step to build resilience in practical, achievable ways. Whether it's juggling family responsibilities, navigating career transitions, or managing daily stress, resilience equips you to stay grounded and thrive.

No matter your circumstances, resilience empowers you to:

- **Adapt to Change:** Navigate life's unpredictability with confidence and flexibility.

- **Turn Setbacks into Opportunities:** See challenges not as barriers but as chances to grow personally and professionally.

- **Maintain Balance and Focus:** Manage stress effectively, enabling you to prioritize what truly matters without losing sight of your goals.

- **Continue Long-Term Growth:** Embrace challenges as opportunities to evolve and build a more fulfilling, sustainable life.

These benefits don't stop with you. Resilience creates a ripple effect that strengthens your relationships, enhances your environment, and inspires fulfillment. With each step forward, you'll uncover strategies to thrive in eight interconnected areas of wellness, discovering how progress in one area positively impacts the others. Resilience allows you to live with intention, balance, and purpose.

Take a moment to reflect on these questions:

- *What's one specific challenge you're facing right now where resilience could make a difference?*

- *How might a resilient mindset change the way you approach this challenge?*

This book provides the tools you need to strengthen your resilience step by step. With each chapter, you'll gain practical strategies to thrive, building a foundation of balance, strength, and fulfillment.

Your journey begins here. Let this be your opportunity to embrace the power of resilience and reshape your life—one intentional step at a time.

Is This Book For You? Identifying Your Path

This book is for anyone ready to take control of their well-being, avoid burnout, and build a purposeful, balanced, and fulfilling life. Resilience isn't a one-size-fits-all solution, it's deeply personal and adaptable to your unique challenges, goals, and lifestyle.

Whether you're seeking clarity, balance, renewed motivation, or simply a fresh perspective, this book provides practical tools and strategies to help you navigate life's demands with confidence.

You may see yourself in one or more of these scenarios:

- **Students** balancing coursework, relationships, and personal growth while struggling to stay focused, manage stress, and avoid burnout. If you're overwhelmed by deadlines or seeking better time management, resilience can help you build sustainable academic and personal success.

- **Entrepreneurs** navigating the uncertainties of running a business, managing risk, and staying motivated while juggling countless responsibilities. If you're feeling stretched thin, resilience strategies can help you maintain productivity, prevent burnout, and keep your vision alive.

- **Parents** managing the endless responsibilities of raising children while balancing career, relationships, and self-care. If you're struggling to find time for yourself without guilt, resilience can help you create harmony in your daily life.

- **Caregivers** supporting loved ones while trying to maintain their own well-being. If you often put others before yourself and feel emotionally drained, resilience can help you set healthy boundaries and preserve your energy.

- **Professionals** looking to grow in their careers while maintaining personal fulfillment. If you're struggling with workplace stress, decision fatigue, or work-life balance, resilience can provide tools to excel in your career without sacrificing well-being.

- **Teachers and Educators** who invest their energy into helping others learn while trying to sustain their own passion and mental well-being. If you're feeling drained, resilience can help you protect your enthusiasm for teaching and avoid burnout.

- **Managers and Team Leaders** guiding teams, making tough decisions, and striving to maintain leadership while fostering a positive work culture. If you feel the weight of responsibility, resilience can help you manage stress while supporting those you lead.

- **Creative Artists or Content Creators** who rely on inspiration, originality, and consistency while navigating the pressures of visibility and performance. If burnout is affecting your creative flow, resilience can help you maintain motivation and prevent exhaustion.

- **Health Enthusiasts** striving to integrate holistic well-being into their daily routines. If you want to improve your mental, emotional, and physical resilience, this book provides strategies to reinforce overall well-being.

- **Lifelong Learners** eager to grow, improve, and challenge themselves continuously. If you value self-development but struggle with focus, self-discipline, or follow-through, resilience can help you stay engaged and motivated.

- **Retirees** transitioning into a new phase of life and searching for purpose, fulfillment, and stability. If you're adjusting to a different pace and looking for meaningful ways to stay active and engaged, resilience can help you shape this new chapter.

- **Young Adults** stepping into independence, building careers, and navigating relationships while learning to balance responsibilities. If you feel overwhelmed by the uncertainty of adult life, resilience can help you develop confidence, adaptability, and direction.

- **Busy Multi-taskers** managing multiple roles and responsibilities, from work and family to personal ambitions. If you constantly feel like there's never enough time, resilience strategies can help you prioritize, set boundaries, and prevent exhaustion.

- **Community-Minded Individuals** dedicated to helping others, advocating for change, or supporting causes close to their hearts. If you pour yourself into others but struggle with balance, resilience can help you maintain your energy while continuing to make a positive impact.

- **Anyone Feeling Overwhelmed** who wants to regain clarity, joy, and balance in everyday life. If stress, uncertainty, or exhaustion are taking over, resilience will help you reclaim control and move forward with confidence.

No matter where you are in life, resilience is the key to navigating challenges, avoiding burnout, and building a sustainable, fulfilling future.

This book provides a clear roadmap for meaningful change by focusing on the eight areas of human wellness: Physical, Intellectual, Emotional, Financial, Occupational, Social, Spiritual, and Environmental. These interconnected areas form the foundation of resilience—strengthening even one can create a ripple effect that enhances every aspect of your well-being.

Your journey toward lasting balance and fulfillment starts now. Keep reading to take control of your growth and build a life rooted in resilience, purpose, and strength.

The 8 Areas of Wellness: Building a Balanced Life

Resilience is most effective when it's holistic. That's why this book focuses on eight interconnected areas of human wellness. Together, these areas form the foundation of a balanced and fulfilling life. When even one area is neglected, it can create stress that ripples through the others. But when all eight are nurtured, they work together to support your resilience and overall well-being.

Think about your own life as you explore the list below.

- *Which areas feel strong?*

- *Where do you see room for growth?*

Before diving into each area, take a moment to reflect on your starting point. Building resilience begins with self-awareness, and this process isn't about starting from scratch. It's about recognizing what's already working in your life while identifying areas where there's room for growth. By understanding your strengths and opportunities, you'll lay the foundation for meaningful progress and a more balanced, resilient life.

Identifying Your Wellness Starting Point

Each person's wellness journey is unique and identifying where you currently stand will help you make more intentional choices moving forward.

- *What's going well for you right now?*

- *Where do you feel the most out of balance in your life?*

- *What's one small step you can take today to create more harmony?*

Recognizing your strengths is just as important as acknowledging areas that need attention. Maybe you already prioritize physical wellness with regular exercise but struggle with maintaining financial stability. Or perhaps you have strong social connections but often neglect emotional self-care.

There's no right or wrong place to start—only the awareness that allows you to move forward with clarity.

With this reflection in mind, let's explore each of the eight areas of wellness and how they work together to support your resilience.

1. Physical Wellness

Building resilience in physical wellness involves prioritizing habits like regular exercise, proper nutrition, and consistent sleep. These practices maintain energy levels, prevent illness, and enable you to recover effectively from physical stress. Physical resilience serves as the foundation for a thriving life, giving you the strength and vitality to manage challenges and pursue your goals.

Take a moment to assess:

- *Do you feel energized throughout the day, or do you often experience fatigue?*

- *Are you consistently making choices that support your physical well-being?*

2. Intellectual Wellness

Resilience in intellectual wellness is about fostering a curious mindset and engaging in lifelong learning. It involves embracing challenges, solving problems creatively, and adapting to new ideas or situations. Strengthening your intellectual resilience equips you to think critically, make informed decisions, and continuously grow.

Consider:

- *When was the last time you intentionally learned something new?*

- *Do you feel mentally stimulated, or are you stuck in a routine that lacks intellectual challenge?*

3. Emotional Wellness

Emotional resilience involves developing emotional regulation, self-awareness, and mental fortitude. These skills empower you to navigate stress, process setbacks, and maintain a positive outlook. By building emotional wellness, you can strengthen relationships, make better decisions, and approach life's ups and downs with confidence.

Ask yourself:

- *How do you typically handle stress or setbacks?*

- *Do you have healthy coping mechanisms in place?*

4. Financial Wellness

Resilience in financial wellness focuses on managing resources wisely, planning for the future, and reducing stress caused by money concerns. It includes understanding the difference between needs and wants, practicing mindful spending, and creating financial security. Building financial resilience allows you to approach challenges with clarity and stability.

Reflect on:

- *Do you feel financially stable, or is money a major source of stress?*

- *Are you actively working toward financial security and long-term stability?*

5. Occupational Wellness

Occupational resilience means balancing work and personal life, finding purpose in your career, and staying adaptable to workplace challenges. Whether you're pursuing growth in your field or seeking fulfillment in your work, occupational wellness ensures your career supports—rather than hinders—your overall well-being.

Think about:

- *Do you find meaning and fulfillment in your work?*

- *Are you setting healthy boundaries to maintain balance?*

6. Social Wellness

Building resilience in social wellness focuses on nurturing supportive relationships, resolving conflicts constructively, and expanding your social network. Social resilience also includes being mindful about how social media impacts your interactions, ensuring that your connections—both online and offline—enhance your life and well-being.

Ask yourself:

- *Do you feel genuinely connected to the people in your life?*

- *Are your relationships supportive, or do they drain your energy?*

7. Spiritual Wellness (This is not about religion)

Resilience in spiritual wellness involves connecting with your values, finding purpose, and cultivating hope and a positive perspective. It's about aligning your actions with what truly matters to you, helping you navigate challenges with confidence and fostering inner peace, whether or not religion is part of your life.

Consider:

- *Do you feel a sense of purpose in your daily life?*

- *What practices help you feel grounded and connected to something bigger than yourself?*

8. Environmental Wellness (Your Personal Space)

Strengthening resilience in environmental wellness begins with creating a safe, organized, and nurturing personal space. By maintaining comfort, functionality, and sensory balance, you can reduce stress and foster an environment that supports your physical and emotional well-being. Your personal space serves as both a retreat and a source of empowerment.

Take a moment to reflect:

- *Does your physical space support or hinder your well-being?*

- *What small changes could improve your environment for greater comfort and focus?*

Thoughts on the 8 Areas of Wellness

Each of these areas is interconnected, meaning progress in one often creates a ripple effect, improving the others. For example: improving your physical wellness can boost your energy and focus, which supports intellectual and occupational growth. Enhancing your emotional resilience can strengthen your relationships, improving your social and spiritual well-being.

By nurturing all eight areas, you'll create a balanced life where resilience becomes second nature. But understanding these areas is just the beginning. What matters most is how you put this knowledge into action.

How to Use This Book

This book is your step-by-step guide to building resilience across the eight interconnected areas of wellness. Whether you're seeking balance, clarity, or personal growth, it offers practical tools to help you thrive in a way that's meaningful and personal to your unique journey.

You don't have to read this book cover to cover in one sitting. Each chapter stands alone, allowing you to begin with the area of wellness that resonates most with your current challenges or goals. Progress in one area of resilience naturally creates a ripple effect, enhancing others and supporting overall growth.

Throughout this book, you'll meet Alex, who navigates challenges across the eight areas of wellness. Alex's experiences provide practical, real-world examples of how small, intentional changes can lead to meaningful growth, offering inspiration as you apply these strategies to your own life.

What to Expect

Each chapter in this book is designed to guide you through one of the eight interconnected areas of wellness, offering a roadmap to help you build resilience step by step. Here's what you'll find in each chapter:

- **Core Components**: Explore the foundational principles that define resilience in the chapter's specific area of wellness.

- **Practical Strategies**: Discover actionable steps you can implement immediately to develop habits that strengthen your resilience.

- **Challenges and Solutions**: Learn about common obstacles you might face and how to overcome them with realistic, proven approaches.

- **Advanced Tips and Insights**: Dive deeper into techniques and practices that further enhance your resilience.

- **Broader Impact**: See how growth in this area creates ripple effects, positively influencing other areas of your life.

- **Scenario:** Discover how the strategies come to life through real-world examples, illustrated by Alex's journey across the eight areas of wellness.

- **Reflection Activities**: Engage in thought-provoking exercises that help you connect the material to your unique circumstances and goals.

This book isn't just about overcoming obstacles, it's about uncovering opportunities for growth and transformation. Each chapter equips you with tools to turn setbacks into stepping stones and create meaningful, lasting change.

As you explore these chapters, remember that progress happens one small step at a time. Start where it feels most relevant to you and let Alex's story inspire you to take intentional steps toward a more resilient and fulfilling life.

Practical Tips for Your Resilience Journey

Your journey through this book is entirely your own. Here's how you can make the most of it:

1. **Start Where You Need It Most**: Identify the area of wellness that feels most out of balance or presents the greatest challenge right now. Begin there and work outward, exploring other chapters as you're ready.

2. **Engage with Reflection Activities**: These exercises are designed to deepen your connection to the material and encourage self-awareness, helping you implement strategies that resonate with your goals.

3. **Draw Inspiration from Alex's Story**: Alex's journey across the eight areas of wellness provides relatable examples of how resilience strategies can create positive change. Use these examples to guide your own steps toward balance and growth.

4. **Take Your Time**: Resilience is not a race. Focus on making small, consistent changes that build lasting habits over time.

By following these steps, you'll gain the clarity, confidence, and practical tools needed to navigate the challenges in your life. Let this book be your companion, guiding you toward a more balanced and fulfilling journey of resilience.

What This Book Is (and Isn't)

This book is a practical guide to creating a balanced, fulfilling, and resilient life. It offers actionable advice, relatable examples, and tools you can use to strengthen your well-being across all eight areas of wellness.

However, it's important to recognize what this book is not. While it's filled with insights and strategies, it's not a substitute for professional therapy, financial advising, or medical care. Some challenges may require specialized guidance, and seeking professional support is a key part of building resilience.

For those ready to deepen their journey, additional resources are available:

- **Online Courses**: Explore in-depth strategies and tools for each area of wellness through my courses, available on my website, Unfryd.com.

- **Future Books**: Keep an eye out for follow-up books that provide an even closer look at each area of wellness.

- **Practical Tools**: Throughout the chapters, you'll find visualization exercises and other resources to guide your progress.

This book isn't about perfection, it's about progress.

By committing to this journey, you'll uncover the clarity, confidence, and strength needed to create lasting change in your life.

As you embark on this journey, remember that resilience isn't about avoiding challenges or striving for an idealized version of yourself. It's about making intentional, meaningful choices that foster balance, growth, and fulfillment. Whether you're reading this book on your own, integrating its lessons into a classroom setting, or using it to inspire others, each chapter is designed as a stepping stone—guiding you to develop habits that support your well-being for the long term.

Before moving forward, take a moment to reflect on where you are right now.

Recognizing Your Strengths and Growth Areas

By picking up this book, you've already taken the first step toward meaningful change. Chances are, you're already thriving in certain areas of wellness—whether it's maintaining strong relationships, managing your time effectively, or staying active and healthy. These successes, no matter how small, provide a foundation to build upon.

At the same time, it's just as valuable to identify areas that feel out of balance. Maybe stress has crept into your daily life, leaving you feeling exhausted. Perhaps financial planning or social connections have taken a backseat to other priorities. It takes courage to look at these areas honestly, but this self-awareness is a critical first step toward lasting growth.

Take a moment to reflect:

- *What areas of wellness feel strongest for you right now?*

- *Which areas feel most out of balance or challenging?*

- *If you could make one change today, what would it be?*

Now that you've reflected on where you are, let's take it a step further. A personal wellness inventory will help you pinpoint exactly where you feel strong, where you may need support, and which areas deserve more attention. This simple exercise isn't about judgment, it's about clarity. By understanding where you stand today, you'll create a starting point for meaningful progress.

Your Personal Wellness Inventory

Use the following questions to evaluate your starting point and set the stage for growth:

- **What areas of wellness feel strongest for you right now?** Celebrate these successes, they're proof of the resilience you've already developed.

- **Which areas feel most out of balance or challenging?** These are opportunities for growth and transformation.

- **If you could make one change today, what would it be?** This small action can be the first step toward building greater resilience.

Write your reflections down, even if they're just a few bullet points. This simple exercise creates clarity and helps you focus on what matters most.

- *Where do you feel the most out of balance in your life right now?*
- *What's one small step you can take today to create more harmony?*

Achieving balance is a journey, and this book will provide the tools and strategies to help you along the way.

Your Journey Starts Here

Resilience isn't a destination; it's a lifelong journey of learning, adapting, and growing. By the time you finish this book, you'll have the practical tools and insights to create meaningful changes in your life. You'll gain the clarity and confidence to turn obstacles into opportunities for growth, laying a foundation of strength and balance that supports every area of your well-being.

With small, consistent actions, you can cultivate resilience across all eight areas of wellness—physical, intellectual, emotional, financial, occupational, social, spiritual, and environmental. Every intentional step you take contributes to a more balanced, fulfilling, and resilient life.

Take a deep breath, open your mind, and embrace this moment as the starting point for meaningful transformation. Each chapter will guide you with actionable strategies, relatable examples, and opportunities to reflect on how resilience can shape your life.

As you move forward into Part 2, we'll dive into practical strategies to strengthen your resilience in each of the eight areas of wellness. From cultivating physical vitality and intellectual growth to nurturing emotional strength and creating a supportive personal environment, every chapter offers tools to help you thrive. Together, these strategies will empower you to build a life rooted in purpose, strength, and balance.

Your resilient life begins here—one intentional step at a time.

PART 2
Building Resilience
Across the 8 Areas of Wellness

Physical Wellness
Understanding
Physical Wellness and Resilience

Physical wellness is about caring for your body to maintain optimal health and energy. It encompasses the daily habits that support your physical well-being, such as regular exercise, balanced nutrition, quality sleep, and rest. Physical wellness isn't just about avoiding illness, it's about having the strength, endurance, and flexibility to navigate life's demands with ease.

At its heart, physical resilience is the foundation of a thriving life. It's about more than just being fit, it's about having the energy, strength, and adaptability to overcome life's physical demands and bounce back from challenges. Whether you're climbing stairs, recovering from illness, or simply trying to get through a long day, physical resilience plays a vital role in keeping you moving forward.

Building physical resilience doesn't just enhance your health, it supports all other areas of wellness. When your body feels strong, you're better equipped to manage stress, focus on your goals, and engage meaningfully in relationships. Physical resilience creates a ripple effect, giving you the stamina and clarity to thrive intellectually, emotionally, socially, and beyond.

By investing in physical wellness, you're not only improving your health but also creating the physical capacity to face life's challenges with confidence and vitality. This chapter will guide you through practical strategies to build physical resilience, helping you lay the groundwork for lasting well-being.

The Core Components of Physical Resilience

Exercise

Movement is essential for physical wellness and resilience. Regular physical activity strengthens your muscles, improves cardiovascular health, and supports mental clarity through the release of endorphins. Exercise doesn't have to mean spending hours in a gym, it's about finding what works for you. This could include brisk walking, yoga, cycling, or even playing a sport, you enjoy.

Example: Imagine someone who works a desk job and feels stiff and tired at the end of each day. They decide to start small, taking a 10-minute walk during their lunch break. As they build consistency, they add light strength training two evenings a week and join a weekend yoga class for flexibility and stress relief. Over time, they notice reduced stiffness, increased energy, and a greater ability to focus during work hours. These small, consistent changes transform their physical health and overall well-being.

Nutrition

Good nutrition fuels your body for resilience and recovery. A well-balanced diet provides the vitamins, minerals, and energy your body needs to perform, repair, and thrive. Focus on whole foods like fruits, vegetables, lean proteins, whole grains, and healthy fats. For those following a plant-based or vegan lifestyle, it's especially important to include nutrient-rich foods like legumes, nuts, seeds, tofu, and fortified options to meet your body's needs.

While these are general recommendations based on widely accepted nutritional research, individual needs vary based on factors like age, activity level, and specific health conditions, including food allergies. Always consult a healthcare professional or registered dietitian for personalized advice.

Example: Imagine a busy professional who relies on takeout and vending machine snacks to get through the day. Over time, they feel sluggish, experience frequent energy crashes, and notice a decline in overall health. Deciding to make a change, they begin prepping simple, balanced meals on Sundays, ensuring they have fresh fruits, vegetables, quinoa, lentils, and avocado ready for the week. They also keep healthy snacks like almonds or hummus at their desk. Within weeks, they feel more energized, maintain steady focus throughout the day, and even sleep better at night.

Sleep

Sleep is the cornerstone of recovery and resilience. It's during rest that your body repairs tissues, restores energy, and processes emotions. Without adequate sleep, your ability to manage stress, focus, and make sound decisions diminishes. Aim for 7–9 hours of quality sleep each night, and establish a bedtime routine to promote consistent, restorative rest.

Note: The need for sleep varies from person to person, depending on factors like age, lifestyle, and health conditions.

While this chapter offers general guidance, we recognize that the topic is complex and unique to each individual.

Example: Picture a college student juggling classes, a part-time job, and a demanding workout routine. They often sacrifice sleep to study late into the night, leaving them feeling drained and unfocused during the day. Eventually, they start incorporating a consistent bedtime, cutting back on late-night screen time, and creating a relaxing pre-sleep routine. Within weeks, they wake up feeling more rested, recover faster from workouts, and find their energy and focus dramatically improved throughout the day.

Rest and Recovery

Physical resilience isn't just about activity, it's about knowing when to rest. Taking time to recover allows your body to rebuild and grow stronger. Overtraining or ignoring your body's need for downtime can lead to injuries, fatigue, and burnout. Embrace recovery days as an essential part of your routine.

Example: Consider a weightlifter who trains intensely five days a week, pushing their body to its limits with heavy lifts and high repetitions. Initially, they skip recovery days, believing constant training is the only way to improve. Over time, they begin to experience joint pain, muscle fatigue, and even performance plateaus. Recognizing the signs, they incorporate recovery strategies, such as taking rest days, using foam rollers for muscle release, and prioritizing proper sleep. The result? They return to their workouts feeling stronger, lift heavier weights, and see better results while avoiding burnout or injuries.

Hydration

Proper hydration is a cornerstone of physical resilience. Your body depends on water to regulate temperature, transport nutrients, and maintain energy levels. Even mild dehydration can lead to fatigue, headaches, and decreased performance. Prioritize drinking enough water throughout the day, especially during and after physical activity.

Example: Imagine a basketball player who often forgets to hydrate during practices and games. Over time, they notice frequent muscle cramps, sluggish movements, and a struggle to maintain focus on the court. Once they begin drinking water regularly, carrying a refillable bottle to practices, and incorporating electrolytes after intense sessions, their performance improves dramatically. They find they can play longer, recover faster, and maintain their energy through the entire game.

Practical Strategies for Building Physical Resilience

Physical resilience is the foundation of a thriving life. When your body is strong, energized, and healthy, it supports every other area of wellness, your mind becomes sharper, your emotions steadier, and your daily challenges more manageable. Building physical resilience isn't just about fitness; it's about equipping yourself to handle stress, recover from setbacks, and pursue your goals with vitality and confidence.

By strengthening your physical resilience, you'll experience improved energy levels, better stress management, faster recovery from challenges, and an overall sense of empowerment. A resilient body enhances your focus, lifts your mood, and gives you the stamina to fully engage in every aspect of your life.

Nutrition: Fueling Your Body for Resilience

- **Focus on Balanced Meals:** Eating whole, nutrient-dense foods provides your body with the energy and nutrients it needs to recover and perform well. A balanced meal includes lean proteins, healthy fats, and a variety of colorful fruits and vegetables.
  - **Example:** Instead of skipping breakfast, grab a piece of whole-grain toast with avocado and a boiled egg for a quick, balanced meal that keeps you energized and focused throughout the morning.
- **Hydration Matters:** Drinking enough water supports energy levels, improves focus, and aids physical recovery.
  - **Example:** Carry a reusable water bottle to ensure you drink water throughout the day, especially if you're active.
- **Limit Processed Foods:** Reducing sugar and overly processed items minimizes energy crashes and improves overall health.
  - **Example:** Swap sugary snacks for natural alternatives like almonds, fruit, or yogurt, which keep you fuller for longer and avoid sugar spikes.
- **Start Small:** Begin with manageable changes, like swapping one processed snack per day for something healthier or incorporating a single serving of vegetables into one meal. Small steps lead to big results over time.

Exercise: Building Strength and Stamina

- **Start Small and Build Gradually:** Focus on consistency over intensity. Even 10 minutes of movement a day can create momentum and set the stage for long-term habits.
  - Example: Start with a 10-minute walk during your lunch break or after dinner to clear your mind and improve circulation.
- **Incorporate Strength Training:** Building muscle enhances overall physical resilience, improves posture, and helps prevent injuries.
  - Example: Use simple bodyweight exercises like squats, push-ups, and planks if you don't have access to equipment.
- **Find What Works for You:** Consistency comes from enjoyment. Explore activities you love, whether it's yoga, weightlifting, hiking, martial arts, or even yard work.
  - Example: If the gym feels intimidating, try a group fitness class or start with an outdoor activity like hiking with friends.
- **Listen to Your Body:** Pay attention to physical cues like fatigue, soreness, or hunger. These signals are your body's way of communicating its limits and needs.
  - Example: If you feel overly sore after a workout, adjust your intensity or focus on recovery stretches and light movement the next day.

Sleep Matters, Too!

- **Create a Consistent Sleep Schedule:** Go to bed and wake up at the same time every day, even on weekends. This regulates your body's internal clock and improves the quality of your rest.
  - **Example:** Set a bedtime alarm to remind yourself to start winding down 30 minutes before you plan to sleep.
- **Optimize Your Sleep Environment:** Ensure your bedroom is conducive to restful sleep by keeping it cool, dark, and quiet. Consider blackout curtains, white noise machines, or an eye mask if necessary.
  - **Example:** Replace old pillows and invest in a comfortable mattress that supports good posture during sleep.
- **Limit Caffeine and Electronics Before Bed:** Avoid caffeine and heavy meals 4–6 hours before bedtime. Minimize screen time in the hour leading up to sleep to reduce blue light exposure, which can disrupt melatonin production.
  - **Example:** Replace late-night scrolling with a calming activity like reading or light stretching.
- **Wind Down with a Relaxation Routine:** Develop a pre-sleep ritual to signal your body that it's time to rest. This could include light yoga, meditation, or journaling to clear your mind of stressors.
  - **Example:** Spend 5–10 minutes practicing deep breathing or mindfulness exercises before bed.
- **Address Sleep Disruptors:** Identify and tackle factors that disrupt your sleep, such as snoring, stress, or an

irregular schedule. If needed, seek professional advice for sleep disorders like insomnia or sleep apnea.

  o **Example:** If stress keeps you awake, jot down a to-do list for the next day to ease your mind.

REMINDERS:

These Are Important for Your Success!

- **Start Small:** Begin with manageable changes, like walking for 10 minutes a day or swapping sugary snacks for healthier options. Small steps lead to big results over time.
- **Listen to Your Body:** Pay attention to signals like fatigue, soreness, or hunger. These cues are your body's way of communicating its needs.
- **Find What Works for You:** Enjoyment is key to consistency. Explore activities you love, whether it's yoga, lifting weights, cardio classes, martial arts, hiking, or yard work.

These practical strategies form the foundation of physical resilience, setting the stage for sustained progress and overall wellness. Once these habits are in place, you can amplify your efforts by incorporating additional methods that enhance your health and vitality. By adopting these practices, you'll create a well-rounded approach to physical resilience, ensuring long-term strength and balance.

Let's explore these key strategies to strengthen your journey.

Additional Practical Strategies to Consider

Breathing Techniques

- o **Why It Matters:** Focused breathing not only calms your mind and boosts endurance by improving oxygen delivery to your muscles, but it also enhances mental clarity and helps manage stress—both crucial for overall resilience.
- o **Example:** Practice diaphragmatic breathing by inhaling deeply through your nose, allowing your abdomen to rise, and then exhaling slowly. Alternatively, try box breathing—inhale for 4 counts, hold for 4 counts, exhale for 4 counts, and hold again for 4 counts—to reduce stress and improve focus during moments of high pressure.

Recovery as a Priority

- o **Why It Matters:** Recovery allows your muscles and tissues to heal, making them stronger and more resilient over time. Prioritizing recovery also supports mental and emotional well-being, preventing burnout and keeping you motivated for the long haul.
- o **Example:** Incorporate active recovery days into your routine with light activities like walking, gentle yoga, or foam rolling. Prioritize sleep as a cornerstone of recovery and explore tools like massages or guided meditation to relax both your body and mind.

Setting a Schedule

- o **Why It Matters:** A well-structured schedule eliminates decision fatigue and helps build sustainable routines. By prioritizing wellness activities, you can create long-term consistency that supports not just physical resilience but all areas of your well-being.
- o **Example:** Block out 30 minutes in your calendar each morning or evening for exercise or meal prep. Treat these wellness activities as non-negotiable appointments, just like meetings or errands.

Monitoring Progress

- o **Why It Matters:** Seeing even small progress reinforces your efforts and encourages long-term commitment. Tracking builds confidence and fosters a proactive mindset that ripples into all areas of wellness.
- o **Example:** Keep a wellness journal to log your workouts, meals, and how you feel each day. Alternatively, use apps or wearable devices to track steps, sleep, or activity levels. Celebrate even small wins, like completing an extra set of reps or walking a few more steps than yesterday.

Building Resilience Through Play

- o **Why It Matters:** Play boosts mental and physical well-being while fostering creativity and strengthening social connections. By making fitness enjoyable, play turns wellness into a fun and sustainable habit, not a chore.

- Example: Join a community league for a sport you enjoy, organize a family hike, or try something adventurous like rock climbing or dance classes.

Incorporating Flexibility and Mobility Training

- **Why It Matters:** Flexibility helps you move comfortably through daily tasks, while mobility ensures optimal joint function, reducing everyday aches and preventing long-term discomfort. Together, they support better physical performance and long-term health.
- **Example:** Dedicate 10 minutes at the end of each workout to stretching exercises like hamstring stretches, hip openers, or shoulder rolls. Alternatively, include a weekly yoga or Pilates class to enhance both flexibility and strength in a structured way.

While understanding the core components of physical resilience and adopting practical strategies is essential, it's equally important to recognize the obstacles you might face along the way. By identifying these hurdles, you can equip yourself with the tools to overcome them and stay on track.

Now that you have tools to build physical resilience, let's explore the common obstacles that may arise and how to overcome them.

Obstacles to Building Physical Resilience

Building physical resilience is an ongoing journey, but obstacles—both internal and external—can make it challenging to maintain consistency. However, by recognizing these barriers and applying effective strategies, you can navigate them with confidence and build lasting resilience.

Internal Obstacles:

Time Constraints

Feeling like you don't have enough hours in the day for exercise, meal prep, or rest can hinder progress.

- **Red Flag:** Constantly telling yourself, "I'll start tomorrow," but never finding the time.
- **How to Overcome It:**
  - ➤ **Incorporate Short Bursts of Activity:** Take the stairs, do a 10-minute stretch during work breaks, or walk after meals. Small activities add up over time.
  - ➤ **Streamline Nutrition:** Focus on quick, healthy meal options. Batch-cook proteins and veggies or opt for pre-cut ingredients to save time.
  - ➤ **Prioritize Sleep:** Set a consistent bedtime routine, even if it's just 15 minutes earlier than usual, to ensure rest doesn't get sacrificed.

Lack of Motivation

Staying consistent can feel daunting when progress seems slow or when life gets in the way.

- **Insight Tip:** Think about how wellness impacts your energy, confidence, and productivity.
- **How to Overcome It:**
  - ➢ Set realistic, short-term goals and celebrate small wins.
  - ➢ Find accountability by partnering with a friend or joining a fitness group.
  - ➢ Make it fun by exploring activities you genuinely enjoy, like dancing, hiking, or yoga.

Guilt or Self Doubt

Believing you've failed if you skip a workout or indulge in an unhealthy snack can create a cycle of avoidance.

- **Mindset Tip:** Progress isn't linear; setbacks are part of growth.
- **How to Overcome It:**
  - ➢ Reframe setbacks as learning opportunities. Reflect on what caused the lapse and adjust accordingly.
  - ➢ Focus on consistency over perfection, every effort counts.
  - ➢ Track successes, even small ones, to remind yourself of your progress.

External Obstacles:

Financial Constraints

The perception that wellness is expensive can be discouraging.

- **Quick Fix:** Wellness doesn't have to break the bank. Many solutions are affordable or free.
- **How to Overcome It:**
    - ➢ Explore free or low-cost fitness options like walking, bodyweight exercises, or YouTube workout videos.
    - ➢ Use budget-friendly nutrition options like beans, frozen vegetables, and whole grains.
    - ➢ Utilize apps or community resources for meal planning and fitness tips.

Environmental Factors

A cluttered home, lack of safe outdoor spaces, or unsupportive surroundings can hinder wellness efforts.

- **Efficiency Tip:** Create a dedicated space that supports your goals, even if it's small.
- **How to Overcome It:**
    - ➢ Declutter a corner for exercise or meditation.
    - ➢ Use public parks, trails, or community centers for fitness activities.
    - ➢ Have open conversations with family or roommates about supporting your goals.

Social Influences

Friends, coworkers, or family may unintentionally discourage wellness efforts by inviting unhealthy habits or undermining your goals.

- **Resolution Idea:** Surround yourself with supportive individuals and communicate your priorities.
- **How to Overcome It:**
  - ➤ Share your goals with loved ones and explain why they matter.
  - ➤ Politely decline activities that conflict with your wellness goals or suggest alternatives.
  - ➤ Join wellness communities or classes to connect with like-minded individuals.

A Thought on Physical Wellness Challenges

Physical challenges are a natural part of building resilience, but they don't have to derail your progress. Obstacles such as time constraints, lack of motivation, or the physical toll of daily life may seem daunting, but they also offer opportunities to reassess your priorities and embrace self-care. Resilience isn't about avoiding difficulties—it's about adapting and growing stronger through them.

For example, if you're short on time, consider incorporating a 10-minute walk during your lunch break or stretching while watching your favorite show. Small adjustments like these can energize your body and clear your mind, reinforcing your commitment to physical wellness without feeling overwhelming. Each small step forward builds confidence and reinforces your ability to navigate life's demands with greater energy and vitality.

The journey to physical wellness isn't about achieving perfection, it's about making steady progress and developing habits that support long-term health. As you overcome obstacles, the ripple effect of physical resilience extends far beyond your body. Strength and vitality enhance all eight areas of wellness, improving emotional regulation, intellectual focus, and even social connections.

By embracing challenges as opportunities to thrive, you create a life rooted in resilience, one where physical wellness becomes a foundation for balance, fulfillment, and overall well-being.

Reflection Activity: What's Next?

Take a moment to reflect and ask yourself:

- *What's one obstacle I'm ready to tackle on my physical wellness journey?*

- *Which solution feels most manageable and realistic to implement this week?*

Write down your plan and commit to taking action this week.

By embracing challenges as opportunities to thrive, you lay the groundwork for a life rooted in resilience. Physical wellness is more than just a pathway to better health—it's the foundation for balance and vitality in every area of your life. As your body grows stronger, so does your capacity to handle stress, stay focused, and nurture meaningful relationships. Each step forward strengthens not just your physical self but also your emotional, intellectual, and social resilience.

With these foundations in place, let's explore the broader impact of physical wellness and how it ripples outward to enhance all eight areas of resilience, empowering you to thrive in every aspect of your life.

The Broader Impact of Physical Resilience on the other Areas of Wellness

Physical resilience doesn't exist in isolation, it's the foundation that supports all other areas of wellness. When your body feels strong and energized, it has a positive ripple effect across your life:

- **Intellectual Wellness**: Physical activity enhances mental clarity, focus, and problem-solving skills, which are essential for intellectual growth.
- **Emotional Wellness**: Regular exercise and proper sleep reduce stress hormones and improve mood, making it easier to manage emotions and face challenges calmly.
- **Financial Wellness**: Investing in your physical health through nutritious food and regular exercise can reduce long-term healthcare costs.
- **Occupational Wellness**: A healthy, energized body supports productivity and focus at work, helping you perform at your best.
- **Social Wellness**: Engaging in physical activities with others—like group sports, walking clubs, or yoga classes—strengthens social connections and creates a sense of community.
- **Spiritual Wellness**: Activities like hiking or jogging in nature can foster a sense of peace, purpose, and connection to something greater.
- **Environmental Wellness**: Maintaining an active lifestyle often encourages creating a space that supports physical health, such as a tidy home for exercising or a well-stocked kitchen for healthy eating.

Physical Wellness Scenario

Alex, someone who has been prioritizing work and responsibilities over his health for years, finds himself in a downward spiral. His days are fueled by caffeine, meals often come from fast food, and late nights working lead to inconsistent sleep schedules. Over time, the toll becomes undeniable—he's carrying extra weight, feeling constantly tired, and struggling to stay focused during important tasks. The effects spill over into his personal life: Alex finds himself snapping at loved ones over minor frustrations and feeling distant in his relationships, as the stress of keeping up with life overshadows quality time with family or friends. His confidence takes a hit, too—he feels stuck and overwhelmed, unsure how to break the cycle.

One day, Alex decides it's time to make a change. Instead of trying to overhaul everything at once, he starts small. The first step is setting a consistent bedtime and wake-up schedule, ensuring he gets at least seven hours of sleep every night. After a few weeks, his energy levels improve, and he feels more rested and clear-headed. He even notices he's less irritable, leading to smoother conversations at work and home.

Next, Alex tackles his eating habits. Instead of relying on fast food, he begins meal-prepping simple, healthy options on Sundays—lean proteins, whole grains, and vegetables. This ensures healthy meals are readily available during the week, reducing the temptation for unhealthy options. He starts to feel lighter and more energetic, and even the occasional indulgence feels like a treat rather than a guilty habit.

45

Finally, Alex adds light activity to his routine. A 15-minute morning walk becomes a daily ritual; a chance to clear his mind, boost his mood, and ease into the day. Over time, that walk turns into 30 minutes, and Alex finds himself brainstorming ideas or reflecting on his goals during this quiet, uninterrupted time.

Within months, the changes ripple outward. Alex's energy has returned, his focus has sharpened, and he feels more confident in both his work and personal life. His relationships improve as he becomes more present and less distracted by stress or exhaustion. By making small, consistent changes, Alex builds physical resilience, proving that even from a tough starting point, progress is possible.

Physical Wellness
Conclusion and Reflection Activity

Building physical resilience is a process, not a destination.

As you reflect on your current habits, ask yourself:

- *What is one small change I could make today to improve my physical health?*
- *How can I incorporate movement, nutrition, sleep, or rest into my daily routine in a way that feels manageable?*

Examples to Get Started:

- Could you take a 10-minute walk during lunch or stretch for five minutes in the morning?
- Could you swap one sugary drink for water or add a serving of vegetables to dinner?
- Could you set a consistent bedtime or avoid screens an hour before bed?

Reflection Activity:

Write down your answers and choose one action to focus on this week. Track your progress daily by jotting a quick note:

- *Did I, do it?*
- *How did it make me feel?*

Remember, even small actions can lead to transformative results. Physical resilience isn't just about health, it's about living a life full of energy, focus, and joy.

Always Remember:

As you strengthen your physical resilience, you'll notice improvements in your energy, focus, and even your relationships. This journey benefits not just your body but your overall well-being.

Small changes lead to big transformations. Celebrate every step forward, no matter how small—it's all progress toward a healthier, more resilient you.

Disclaimer: *The strategies outlined in this chapter are designed to support and enhance your overall physical resilience. However, they are not a substitute for professional medical advice, diagnosis, or treatment. Always consult with a healthcare provider, physician, or certified fitness professional before making significant changes to your exercise, nutrition, or wellness routine, especially if you have existing health conditions, injuries, or concerns. The suggestions in this chapter are meant to be general guidelines and should be adapted to fit your personal needs and circumstances.*

Intellectual Wellness

Understanding
Intellectual Wellness and Resilience

Intellectual wellness is about cultivating a curious and open mind. It involves engaging in lifelong learning, critical thinking, and creative exploration to grow your knowledge and skills. Intellectual wellness isn't just about academics, it's about challenging yourself to think in new ways, solve problems, and adapt to an ever-changing world.

In your daily life, intellectual wellness plays a vital role in how you approach challenges, make decisions, and connect with others. Whether you're learning a new skill, exploring innovative ideas, or analyzing information critically, maintaining intellectual wellness empowers you to stay flexible and resourceful.

Building intellectual resilience enhances your ability to adapt when faced with uncertainty or complex problems. It helps you recover from setbacks, rethink assumptions, and approach challenges with confidence and curiosity. Intellectual resilience ensures that your mind remains a powerful tool, even in difficult times.

This chapter will guide you through strategies to strengthen intellectual wellness and resilience. You'll learn how to stay curious, engage in meaningful learning, and embrace the mental flexibility that empowers you to thrive in all areas of life.

The Core Components of Intellectual Wellness

1. Curiosity

Curiosity is the engine of intellectual resilience. It drives you to explore, ask questions, and seek out new information. By staying curious, you keep your mind active and open to new ideas, which helps you adapt to challenges and grow intellectually. Curiosity isn't about having all the answers; it's about being excited to discover them.

Example: A curious person might dive into learning about a new hobby, like painting, asking questions and experimenting with different styles and techniques until they've mastered the basics. This habit keeps their mind sharp and adaptable.

2. Lifelong Learning

Lifelong learning is the commitment to expanding your knowledge and skills throughout your life. It's not limited to formal education, it can include reading, attending workshops, watching tutorials, or learning from experiences. Lifelong learning keeps your mind engaged and enhances your ability to adapt to change.

Example: Someone who dedicates time each month to an online course or self-paced learning not only gains new knowledge but also builds confidence in tackling future challenges.

3. Critical Thinking

Critical thinking is the ability to analyze information, question assumptions, and evaluate situations objectively. It allows you to navigate complex problems, make informed decisions, and adapt your perspective when new information arises.

Example: When presented with conflicting news reports, a critical thinker investigates multiple sources, evaluates their credibility, and forms a balanced conclusion.

4. Adaptability

Adaptability is the intellectual skill of adjusting your thinking when faced with new challenges, ideas, or information. It's about letting go of rigid beliefs and embracing flexibility to solve problems effectively. Adaptable thinkers are better equipped to handle uncertainty and change.

Example: An employee who adapts to using new software at work by watching tutorials and practicing finds themselves thriving in their role rather than feeling overwhelmed.

5. Creative Problem-Solving

Creative problem-solving is the ability to approach challenges with innovation and originality. It involves thinking outside the box, connecting seemingly unrelated ideas, and experimenting with new approaches to find effective solutions. This skill strengthens intellectual resilience by helping you tackle problems from multiple angles.

Example: Someone tasked with organizing a last-minute event uses creative problem-solving to repurpose available resources, turning a potential disaster into a successful gathering.

Practical Strategies for Building Intellectual Resilience

Intellectual resilience is about more than just knowledge, it's about having the flexibility and curiosity to navigate life's complexities, embrace challenges, and continuously grow. It's the ability to adapt your thinking, solve problems creatively, and learn from both success and failure. In a fast-changing world, building intellectual resilience helps you stay confident, capable, and prepared for whatever comes your way.

This section offers practical strategies to strengthen intellectual resilience in ways that are both manageable and impactful, empowering you to think critically, embrace learning, and adapt with confidence.

1. Cultivating Curiosity

Curiosity is the foundation of intellectual resilience. Asking questions, exploring new ideas, and staying open to learning spark creativity and critical thinking.

- **Strategy**: Set a goal to learn something new each day, no matter how small.
  Example: Listen to a podcast on a topic you're unfamiliar with during your lunch hour or commute, ask a colleague about their expertise in an area outside your role.
- **Why It Works**: Curiosity keeps your mind engaged and adaptable, helping you discover new perspectives and solutions.
- **Challenge Yourself**: Take on activities that stretch your mental abilities, like puzzles, learning a new skill, or diving into unfamiliar topics.

2. Lifelong Learning

Continuing to learn throughout life strengthens your mental agility and keeps your brain sharp.

- **Strategy**: Enroll in a course, read books outside your usual interests, or explore new skills.
  Example: A professional signs up for an online class in coding to enhance their career prospects, while a retiree takes a local art class to explore their creative side.
- **Why It Works**: Lifelong learning not only improves intellectual resilience but also boosts confidence in tackling new challenges.
- **Seek Diverse Perspectives**: Engage with people, books, or media that challenge your worldview to expand your thinking.

3. Problem-Solving and Adaptability

Being able to approach challenges with a problem-solving mindset helps you adapt when things don't go as planned.

- **Strategy**: Break problems into smaller, manageable steps, and brainstorm multiple solutions.
  Example: When faced with an unexpected work deadline, prioritize tasks, delegate them when possible, and communicate with your team to find a workable solution.
- **Why It Works**: Problem-solving builds resilience by teaching you to remain calm, flexible, and focused under pressure.

4. Staying Open-Minded

Intellectual resilience thrives when you're willing to listen to differing opinions and reconsider your own beliefs.

- **Strategy:** Practice active listening in conversations, especially with people who hold opposing views.
  Example: During a debate on a controversial topic, instead of arguing, ask thoughtful questions to understand the other person's perspective.
- **Why It Works:** Staying open-minded enhances empathy, broadens your perspective, and fosters creative thinking.

5. Reflection and Self-Awareness

Taking time to reflect on your experiences helps you identify patterns, learn from mistakes, and make intentional improvements.

- **Strategy:** Keep a journal to document your thoughts, decisions, and what you've learned.
  Example: After completing a project, write down what went well, what could improve, and what you'll do differently next time.
- **Why It Works:** Reflection deepens self-awareness, which is essential for personal and intellectual growth.
- **Stay Curious:** Adopt a mindset of *"What can I learn from this?"* in any situation, especially setbacks.

6. Building a "Failure Mindset"

Learn to embrace failure as a natural part of growth and intellectual resilience.

- **Strategy**: After encountering a setback, ask yourself, *"What can I learn from this?"* Analyze what went wrong and identify one takeaway to apply in the future.
  Example: After giving a presentation that didn't land well, reflect on audience feedback, practice delivery, and try a new approach for next time.
- **Why It Works**: Viewing failure as a learning opportunity reduces fear of taking risks and strengthens problem-solving abilities.

7. Expanding Vocabulary and Communication Skills

Improving your vocabulary sharpens your ability to express ideas clearly and understand complex information.

- **Strategy**: Learn one new word daily and use it in conversations or writing.
  Example: Choose words related to your field, like "synergy" or "iteration," or explore unrelated terms to expand your versatility.
- **Why It Works**: Effective communication is a cornerstone of intellectual resilience, helping you connect ideas and collaborate with others.

8. Reducing Cognitive Overload

Managing distractions and information overload preserves mental clarity and focus.

- **Strategy:** Schedule focused, uninterrupted time blocks for deep work, and minimize multitasking.
  Example: Use productivity tools like the Pomodoro Technique, setting a timer for 25 minutes of focused work followed by a 5-minute break.
- **Why It Works:** Reducing cognitive overload improves decision-making and allows you to approach tasks with greater clarity and effectiveness.

Even with curiosity and motivation, building Intellectual Resilience can present unique challenges. These barriers often include internal doubts and external distractions. Recognizing them is the first step toward overcoming them and fostering a mindset of continuous growth.

Obstacles to Building Intellectual Wellness

Developing intellectual wellness can be incredibly rewarding, but like any area of growth, it's not without its challenges. By identifying both internal and external obstacles, you can create strategies to navigate them effectively and continue expanding your intellectual resilience. This section explores common hurdles and provides actionable ways to overcome them.

Internal Obstacles

Fear of Failure

Trying something new or challenging can be intimidating, especially if you fear making mistakes or not succeeding.

- **Red Flag:** Hesitating to tackle a new skill or project because of self-doubt.
- **How to Overcome It:**
  - ➤ Reframe failure as a learning opportunity rather than a setback. Ask, "What can I learn from this experience?"
  - ➤ Start small with manageable goals to build confidence. For example, read one chapter of a book instead of committing to the whole thing at once.
  - ➤ Celebrate incremental progress rather than focusing solely on the end result.

Lack of Time

Busy schedules can make it difficult to prioritize intellectual growth.

- **Insight Tip:** If you feel like there's no time to learn, reflect on whether small adjustments could open up opportunities.
- **How to Overcome It:**
  - ➢ Incorporate learning into your daily routine. Listen to audiobooks during your commute or watch educational videos during breaks.
  - ➢ Dedicate short, focused time blocks to intellectual activities, such as 15 minutes of reading or journaling each day.
  - ➢ Use time management tools to identify and eliminate unnecessary tasks that consume your time.

Mental Fatigue

Constant stress or overwork can make engaging in intellectual activities feel exhausting.

- **Mindset Tip:** Intellectual wellness thrives on curiosity, which is hard to maintain when you're mentally drained.
- **How to Overcome It:**
  - ➢ Prioritize self-care practices, like adequate sleep, physical activity, and mindfulness, to recharge your mental energy.
  - ➢ Alternate between challenging and light intellectual tasks to avoid burnout.
  - ➢ Take intentional breaks to refresh your mind and maintain focus.

External Obstacles

Limited Access to Resources

Not everyone has immediate access to books, courses, or other learning materials.

- Quick Fix: Intellectual growth doesn't always require expensive resources.
- How to Overcome It:
  - ➤ Utilize free or low-cost resources, such as public libraries, online tutorials, or community workshops.
  - ➤ Join local or online learning groups that share knowledge and resources.
  - ➤ Explore free apps or podcasts that offer valuable insights in various fields.

Negative Social Influences

Surrounding yourself with people who discourage curiosity or dismiss intellectual pursuits can stifle growth.

- **Resolution Idea:** Seek out relationships and communities that inspire and challenge you.
- **How to Overcome It:**
  - ➤ Join groups or networks focused on personal development, such as book clubs or professional associations.
  - ➤ Share your learning goals with supportive friends or family members to stay motivated.
  - ➤ Distance yourself from individuals who consistently undermine your efforts.

Overwhelming Information

In today's digital age, the sheer volume of available information can make it difficult to know where to start.

- **Efficiency Tip:** Curate your learning to focus on quality over quantity.
- **How to Overcome It:**
  - ➤ Identify your priorities and set specific learning goals to narrow your focus.
  - ➤ Use reputable sources to avoid misinformation or unproductive rabbit holes.
  - ➤ Limit your intake by scheduling focused time for learning and avoiding multitasking.

A Thought on Intellectual Wellness Challenges

Intellectual challenges are not roadblocks, they're opportunities to expand your mind, sharpen your skills, and foster resilience. Whether it's overcoming a fear of failure, finding time to engage in learning, or staying motivated amidst distractions, each obstacle is a chance to grow. Embracing these challenges is an essential part of intellectual resilience. By viewing setbacks as stepping stones and staying curious, you can develop a stronger, more adaptable mindset that empowers you to navigate life's complexities with confidence and clarity.

Reflection Activity: What's Next?

Take a moment to reflect and ask yourself:

- *What's one internal or external obstacle I've faced in building intellectual resilience?*

- *Which strategy feels most realistic for me to try this week?*

Write down your plan and commit to taking action.

Growth starts with intentional steps, no matter how small!

Now that we've identified common challenges and practical strategies, let's consider how intellectual resilience extends beyond personal growth. Let's explore the broader impact of intellectual wellness and how fostering curiosity and adaptability can positively influence all aspects of your well-being.

The Broader Impact of Intellectual Resilience on the other Areas of Wellness

Intellectual resilience goes beyond learning—it equips you to approach life with curiosity, adaptability, and a growth mindset. Its ripple effect strengthens:

- **Physical Wellness**: Staying mentally sharp encourages making informed decisions about exercise, nutrition, and overall health.
- **Emotional Wellness**: Learning coping strategies and self-awareness through intellectual growth helps you navigate stress and emotional challenges more effectively.
- **Financial Wellness**: A growth mindset can inspire smart financial planning and creative problem-solving for financial challenges.
- **Occupational Wellness**: Intellectual growth boosts professional skills, helping you stay adaptable and competitive in your career.
- **Social Wellness**: Intellectual engagement fosters better communication and deeper conversations, enhancing your relationships and ability to connect with others.
- **Spiritual Wellness**: Exploring new ideas or philosophies can deepen your sense of purpose and alignment with your values.
- **Environmental Wellness**: Applying intellectual resilience to your personal space might mean finding innovative ways to organize or create a calming environment.

Intellectual Wellness Scenario

Alex, our entrepreneur running a small but growing e-commerce business, built his company from scratch, relying on hard work, intuition, and grit. However, as the market evolves, new competitors enter the space with innovative marketing strategies, advanced technology, and data-driven decision-making. Alex, feeling overwhelmed, continues to rely on methods that worked in the past, avoiding new tools and trends out of fear of wasting time or resources. Over time, his business begins to stagnate, sales plateau, and Alex starts losing confidence in his ability to stay competitive.

One day, Alex recognizes the need to adapt and begins to focus on building his intellectual resilience. He starts small, dedicating 20 minutes each morning to reading about industry trends and emerging technologies. He discovers new opportunities in search engine optimization (SEO) and digital marketing and decides to sign up for a short online course on these topics. Though initially challenging, these lessons open the door to strategies that Alex begins implementing in his business.

As Alex becomes more comfortable with innovation, he sets aside time each week to reflect on what's working and what isn't, identifying gaps in his knowledge. He also begins seeking diverse perspectives by joining a local entrepreneurial networking group. Through conversations with fellow business owners, Alex learns creative approaches to growth, from automating processes to leveraging analytics for better customer insights.

Within a few months, Alex's renewed curiosity and adaptability start paying off. His business sees an uptick in online visibility, resulting in higher sales. Alex feels re-energized, no longer bogged down by fear of change, and more confident in navigating future challenges. Inspired by his progress, Alex even starts mentoring other entrepreneurs, sharing the lessons he's learned about embracing intellectual resilience.

On the flip side, neglecting intellectual resilience could have had serious consequences. Without the willingness to adapt and learn, Alex's business might have fallen further behind, leading to financial strain, frustration, and burnout. By embracing a growth mindset, Alex not only strengthens his business but also develops skills that support long-term success and personal fulfillment.

Intellectual Wellness
Conclusion and Reflection Activity

Expanding your intellectual resilience isn't just about gaining knowledge, it's about developing the skills and adaptability to navigate life's challenges with confidence and creativity. When you challenge your mind to grow, you're also strengthening your ability to manage emotions, build relationships, and adapt to changes in your career or personal life. Intellectual resilience is the foundation for thriving in a complex, ever-changing world.

As you reflect on your intellectual habits, ask yourself:

- *When was the last time I actively sought to learn something new?*
- *What's one area of my life where intellectual resilience could help me overcome a challenge?*

Examples to Get Started:

- If you've been struggling with work stress, explore a book or course on time management.
- If you want to expand your perspective, attend a community discussion or engage in a debate on a topic you're passionate about.
- If you enjoy hands-on learning, try a new skill like cooking, coding, or crafting.

Reflection Activity:

Write down one intellectual challenge you'll take on this week. Track your progress by reflecting on these questions:

- *What did I learn?*

- *How did it make me feel?*

- *What's the next step in my journey?*

Always Remember:

Building intellectual resilience doesn't just improve your ability to think critically and adapt—it also enhances your emotional wellness by reducing stress in uncertain situations, strengthens your occupational wellness by improving problem-solving skills, and even contributes to social wellness by fostering better communication and empathy.

Every small step you take to challenge your mind strengthens your ability to navigate life's complexities with resilience and confidence. Celebrate your curiosity—it's one of your greatest strengths.

Disclaimer: *The strategies in this section are designed to enhance intellectual resilience and adaptability. However, they are not a substitute for professional advice in situations that require expert guidance, such as educational planning, career counseling, or mental health concerns. If you're facing significant challenges in these areas, consider consulting with a qualified professional to develop a customized approach that meets your needs.*

Emotional Wellness

Understanding
Emotional Wellness and Resilience

Emotional wellness is about understanding, managing, and expressing your emotions in healthy and constructive ways. It encompasses self-awareness, emotional regulation, and the ability to navigate relationships and challenges with empathy and balance. Emotional wellness doesn't mean always being happy, it means being able to process and respond to emotions effectively.

Your emotional wellness impacts how you handle stress, overcome setbacks, and connect with others. It influences your confidence, mental clarity, and ability to stay grounded in difficult situations. By cultivating emotional wellness, you can experience life's highs and lows with greater clarity and purpose.

Building emotional resilience deepens your ability to recover from stress and adapt to challenges. It enables you to view setbacks as opportunities for growth, remain calm under pressure, and foster strong, supportive relationships. Emotional resilience creates a sense of stability and confidence that extends into every part of your life.

In this chapter, you'll discover strategies to enhance emotional wellness and resilience. From mindfulness to emotional regulation techniques, you'll gain tools to navigate life's challenges with strength, clarity, and compassion.

The Core Components of Emotional Wellness

1. Self-Awareness

Self-awareness is the foundation of emotional wellness. It's the ability to recognize your emotions, understand their triggers, and assess how they influence your thoughts and actions. By becoming more self-aware, you can identify patterns in your emotional responses and take control of how you react to life's challenges.

Example: Someone who notices they feel irritable before important meetings learns to address their nerves by practicing deep breathing beforehand, improving their confidence and communication.

2. Emotional Regulation

Emotional regulation is the ability to manage your emotions in a healthy and constructive way. It doesn't mean suppressing your feelings, it means finding ways to express and process them effectively. Emotional regulation helps you respond thoughtfully in moments of tension, avoid unnecessary conflicts, and maintain emotional balance in your relationships.

Example: During a heated conversation with their partner, someone feels frustration building. Instead of reacting impulsively, they take a moment to pause, breathe, and choose their words carefully. This allows them to express their feelings without escalating the situation, creating space for a productive and respectful dialogue.

3. Empathy

Empathy is the ability to understand and share the feelings of others. It strengthens connections, deepens relationships, and fosters compassion. Practicing empathy not only helps you support others but also enhances your emotional intelligence by allowing you to see situations from another person's perspective.

Example: A friend shares that they're feeling overwhelmed with work and family responsibilities. Instead of offering quick advice or dismissing their concerns, someone practices empathy by truly listening and acknowledging how stressful the situation must feel. They respond with kindness, saying, *"That sounds like a lot to handle. I'm here if you need someone to talk to."* This simple act of understanding helps their friend feel supported and valued.

4. Optimism

Optimism is the practice of focusing on possibilities rather than obstacles. It's not about ignoring difficulties but about believing in your ability to overcome them. Optimism helps you maintain hope and motivation, even in challenging times, and supports emotional resilience by reducing the impact of negative thoughts.

Example: Imagine someone facing a setback, such as not getting the promotion they were hoping for. Instead of dwelling on disappointment, they focus on how this gives them time to refine their skills, seek feedback, and explore new opportunities. By reframing the situation, they use optimism to stay motivated, realizing this is a stepping stone rather than a dead end.

5. Healthy Boundaries

Healthy boundaries are essential for protecting your emotional wellness. They involve setting clear limits with others to ensure your needs and well-being are respected. Boundaries help prevent emotional exhaustion, reduce stress, and create space for meaningful relationships.

Example: Someone who regularly receives late-night work emails establishes a boundary by turning off notifications after 7 p.m., prioritizing their personal time and mental health.

Practical Strategies for Building Emotional Resilience

Emotional resilience is the ability to navigate life's ups and downs with confidence and composure. It allows you to handle stress, setbacks, and challenges without becoming overwhelmed. By strengthening emotional resilience, you can cultivate healthier relationships, better decision-making, and a deeper sense of inner peace. This section provides actionable strategies to help you manage emotions effectively, maintain a positive outlook, and build lasting resilience.

1. Practice Mindfulness

Mindfulness helps you tune into your emotions and respond to challenges with clarity rather than reacting impulsively.

- **Strategy**: Spend a few minutes each day practicing mindfulness techniques, such as deep breathing, meditation, or journaling.
  Example: Begin your morning with five minutes of focused breathing to set a calm tone for the day.
- **Why It Works**: Mindfulness increases self-awareness, helping you recognize and regulate your emotions in the moment.

2. Reframe Challenges

The way you perceive challenges can greatly influence your emotional response. Reframing helps you view difficulties as opportunities for growth.

- **Strategy:** When faced with a setback, ask yourself, *"What's one thing I can learn from this experience?"* **Example:** If you miss an important deadline, reflect on what changes in time management or communication could prevent it in the future.
- **Why It Works:** Reframing shifts your mindset from frustration to problem-solving, reducing stress and fostering optimism.

3. Build a Support Network

Strong relationships provide a buffer against stress and a source of encouragement during tough times.

- **Strategy:** Surround yourself with people who uplift and support you and make time to connect regularly. **Example:** Schedule a weekly check-in with a trusted friend or join a community group where you can share experiences and advice.
- **Why It Works:** A supportive network helps you feel less isolated and more capable of handling emotional challenges.

4. Practice Emotional Regulation

Emotional regulation involves understanding and managing your feelings, especially in high-stress situations.

- **Strategy**: Pause and name your emotions when you feel overwhelmed, such as *"I'm feeling frustrated because…"* This creates space to think before reacting.
  Example: During a heated conversation, take a deep breath and identify the root of your frustration before responding.
- **Why It Works**: Emotional regulation helps you respond thoughtfully instead of reacting impulsively, improving relationships and outcomes.

5. Cultivate Gratitude

Gratitude shifts your focus from what's lacking to what's going well, fostering emotional resilience.

- **Strategy**: Write down three things you're grateful for every day, no matter how small.
  Example: At the end of the day, reflect on simple joys like a kind gesture, a completed task, or a delicious meal.
- **Why It Works**: Gratitude rewires your brain to notice positives, improving emotional balance and reducing stress.

6. Develop Self-Compassion

Self-compassion is about treating yourself with kindness and understanding, especially during difficult times.

- **Strategy:** When you make a mistake, speak to yourself as you would a close friend, offering encouragement instead of criticism.
  Example: Instead of saying, *"I can't believe I failed,"* try, *"This didn't go as planned, but I'll learn and improve next time."*
- **Why It Works:** Self-compassion reduces negative self-talk and helps you bounce back from setbacks more quickly.

Emotional Resilience is a vital part of overall wellness, but even with the best intentions, challenges can arise. These obstacles may include internal struggles with self-regulation or external stressors from your environment, but they don't have to derail your progress. By addressing these challenges head-on, you can cultivate emotional balance and strength.

Obstacles to Building Emotional Wellness

Building emotional wellness requires self-awareness, patience, and intentionality. Challenges in this area often stem from both internal struggles and external pressures. By recognizing these obstacles, you can take meaningful steps to address them and create lasting emotional resilience in your life.

Internal Obstacles

Difficulty Identifying Emotions

Struggling to recognize or articulate feelings can lead to frustration or emotional suppression.

- **Insight Tip:** Emotional awareness is the first step to emotional regulation. If you're unsure what you're feeling, pause and reflect.
- **How to Overcome It:**
  - ➢ Practice journaling to explore your emotions in a safe space.
  - ➢ Use an emotion wheel or list to label your feelings and identify their root causes.
  - ➢ Incorporate mindfulness practices to tune into your emotions without judgment.

Negative Self-Talk

Persistent critical or pessimistic thoughts can undermine confidence and emotional well-being.

- Mindset Tip: Pay attention to your internal dialogue—it shapes your reality and emotional state.
- How to Overcome It:

➢ Reframe negative thoughts by questioning their accuracy and replacing them with constructive affirmations.
➢ Celebrate small wins to shift focus from shortcomings to progress.
➢ Surround yourself with positive influences that reinforce optimism and self-compassion.

Fear of Vulnerability

Hesitation to share feelings or seek help can lead to isolation and emotional stagnation.

- **Red Flag:** Avoiding emotional conversations or resisting support from others during tough times.
- **How to Overcome It:**
  ➢ Start small by opening up to someone you trust about a minor concern.
  ➢ Join support groups or workshops where vulnerability is normalized and encouraged.
  ➢ Practice self-reflection to build confidence in expressing your feelings authentically.

External Obstacles

Toxic Relationships

Interactions with unsupportive or harmful individuals can drain emotional energy and hinder resilience.

- **Quick Fix:** Evaluate the quality of your relationships and prioritize those that uplift you.
- **How to Overcome It:**
  - ➤ Set boundaries with people who exhibit toxic behaviors.
  - ➤ Focus on building connections with individuals who encourage your growth.
  - ➤ Seek professional guidance to navigate complex or difficult relationships.

Unpredictable Stressors

Unexpected events, like job loss or family emergencies, can overwhelm emotional reserves.

- **Efficiency Tip:** Emotional resilience thrives on preparedness and adaptability.
- **How to Overcome It:**
  - ➤ Build a toolkit of coping strategies, such as deep breathing, meditation, or grounding exercises.
  - ➤ Lean on your support network during times of uncertainty.
  - ➤ Acknowledge the fact that not all stressors can be controlled, but your response to them can be.

Overcommitment

Taking on too many responsibilities without leaving time for self-care can lead to emotional burnout.

- **Resolution Idea:** Learn to say "no" when necessary and prioritize your well-being.
- **How to Overcome It:**
  - ➤ Evaluate your commitments and delegate or decline tasks that aren't essential.
  - ➤ Schedule downtime into your calendar as intentionally as work or social events.
  - ➤ Practice self-compassion when prioritizing your needs over others' expectations.

A Thought on Emotional Wellness Challenges

Emotions can be complex, especially during challenging times, but facing these difficulties head-on is essential to building emotional resilience. Emotional resilience isn't about avoiding hardship; it's about understanding your feelings, embracing your vulnerabilities, and using setbacks as stepping stones for personal growth. The challenges you face in cultivating emotional resilience aren't roadblocks, they're opportunities to deepen self-awareness, develop coping strategies, and emerge stronger. By approaching these obstacles with intentionality and practical solutions, you can foster emotional balance, strengthen your inner resolve, and experience greater fulfillment in all areas of life.

Reflection Activity: What's Next?

Take a moment to reflect and ask yourself:

- *What's one emotional wellness obstacle I'm ready to tackle?*

- *Which solution feels most realistic to implement this week?*

Write down your plan and commit to trying it.

Small, intentional changes can lead to lasting emotional strength and resilience.

Having addressed obstacles and their solutions, it's time to reflect on the profound ripple effect emotional resilience can have. Let's explore the broader impact of emotional wellness and how strengthening emotional regulation and awareness supports every area of your life.

The Broader Impact of Emotional Resilience on the other Areas of Wellness

Emotional resilience helps you manage stress, maintain balance, and respond to challenges with grace. Its influence extends to:

- **Physical Wellness**: Regulating emotions reduces stress levels, supporting better sleep, digestion, and overall physical health.
- **Intellectual Wellness**: Emotional regulation clears mental clutter, making it easier to focus, learn, and think critically.
- **Financial Wellness**: Emotional stability can lead to better decision-making about spending and saving, reducing financial stress.
- **Occupational Wellness**: Emotional resilience allows you to handle workplace stress and setbacks with confidence and adaptability.
- **Social Wellness**: Building emotional resilience improves communication, empathy, and conflict resolution, strengthening your relationships.
- **Spiritual Wellness**: Emotional awareness can deepen your connection to your values and help you align with your sense of purpose.
- **Environmental Wellness**: Managing emotions fosters a desire for organization and calm in your surroundings, creating a nurturing space.

Emotional Wellness Scenario

Alex, an entrepreneur navigating the fast-paced world of running an e-commerce business, finds his days packed with juggling orders, managing customer concerns, and strategizing to stay ahead of competitors. Recently, the constant demands have begun to take a toll. The smallest setbacks—a delayed shipment or a negative review—feel like personal failures, fueling frustration and self-doubt. Instead of addressing these emotions, Alex brushes them aside to "stay productive," but this avoidance creates a simmering tension that starts spilling over into personal relationships. He snaps at loved ones over minor issues, feels increasingly isolated, and struggles to maintain meaningful connections.

Recognizing the growing impact of his emotional struggles, Alex decides to focus on building emotional resilience. He begins with small but impactful changes, starting each day with five minutes of focused breathing. This mindfulness practice helps Alex center himself before diving into work, creating a sense of calm and focus that carries into the rest of his day. Over time, Alex notices that this habit reduces his reactive outbursts and helps him approach challenges with a clearer, more composed mindset.

Alex also starts reframing challenges. When a major shipment is delayed, instead of spiraling into frustration, he asks himself, "What's one proactive step I can take to fix this?" By focusing on solutions rather than problems, Alex gains confidence in his ability to adapt and finds his stress levels decreasing. This mindset shift not only helps him professionally but also allows him to approach personal challenges with more patience and understanding.

Recognizing the value of connection, Alex joins a local entrepreneurial group. The group becomes a safe space where they can share frustrations, celebrate wins, and gain fresh perspectives. Through this network, Alex learns the importance of sharing his burdens instead of carrying them alone. The camaraderie and support from like-minded individuals create a sense of balance and mutual encouragement.

Over time, Alex notices profound changes. The morning ritual of mindfulness, reframing techniques, and the supportive connections he has built lead to fewer emotional meltdowns and greater clarity when facing tough decisions. Alex feels more in control, both in his business and personal life. He finds that he is better equipped to navigate challenges while strengthening bonds with loved ones and rediscovering joy in his entrepreneurial journey.

Had Alex neglected emotional resilience, the pressure might have continued to build. Emotional outbursts could have alienated collaborators, strained relationships, and amplified self-doubt. This could have spiraled into burnout, threatening both his business and personal well-being. Instead, by fostering emotional resilience, Alex gains the tools to face life's challenges with confidence and grace, improving not just his business but his overall quality of life.

Emotional Wellness
Conclusion and Reflection Activity

Strengthening your emotional resilience doesn't mean avoiding stress or setbacks—it means learning to navigate them with grace, strength, and confidence. Emotional resilience empowers you to stay grounded during challenges, process your emotions effectively, and bounce back stronger.

Take a moment to reflect on your emotional habits. Ask yourself:

- *How do I typically respond to stress or setbacks?*

- *What's one small step I could take to strengthen my emotional resilience?*

Examples to Get Started:

- If stress leaves you feeling overwhelmed, try journaling for five minutes each morning and evening to organize your thoughts and emotions.
- If you find it hard to focus on positives, start a gratitude practice by listing three things you're thankful for each evening and then again in the morning.
- If setbacks feel isolating, reach out to a friend or loved one for support and perspective.

Reflection Activity:

Write down one emotional resilience strategy to try this week. At the end of the week, reflect on these questions:

- *How did this strategy help me handle stress or setbacks?*

- *Did it change the way I view challenges?*

- *What's the next small step I can take to continue building my emotional resilience?*

Always Remember:

As you strengthen your emotional resilience, you'll notice its positive effects ripple into other areas of your life. Your relationships may become more fulfilling, your focus sharper, and your overall sense of well-being more balanced. Emotional resilience is the foundation for thriving in all aspects of life.

Every small step you take builds your capacity to handle life's ups and downs with greater ease and confidence. Celebrate your progress, it's proof of your growing resilience and your commitment to a more balanced, fulfilling life.

Disclaimer: The strategies in this section are designed to help you build emotional resilience and navigate everyday challenges. However, they are not a substitute for therapy, counseling, or professional mental health support. If you're experiencing significant emotional distress, trauma, or mental health concerns, please consult a qualified professional to develop a personalized plan for your well-being.

Financial Wellness

Understanding
Financial Wellness and Resilience

Financial wellness is about managing your resources effectively to achieve stability, security, and peace of mind. It involves budgeting, saving, planning for the future, and making informed decisions about your financial goals. Financial wellness isn't defined by how much money you have but by how well you manage it to support your well-being.

In your daily life, financial wellness reduces stress and allows you to focus on what truly matters. When you're financially stable, you can pursue opportunities, handle unexpected expenses, and feel more in control of your life. Financial wellness is not just about money, it's about creating the freedom to live in alignment with your values.

Building financial resilience strengthens your ability to adapt to financial challenges, whether it's an unexpected expense, a shift in income, or a major life transition. It empowers you to handle adversity with confidence and maintain a sense of control over your financial future.

This chapter will explore practical strategies for building financial wellness and resilience. You'll learn how to create a budget, save for emergencies, and make decisions that support your financial and overall well-being.

The Core Components of Financial Wellness

1. Budgeting and Planning

Budgeting and planning form the foundation of financial wellness. A budget gives you a clear picture of your income, expenses, and financial goals, empowering you to make informed decisions. By tracking your spending and setting realistic limits, you can allocate resources effectively and reduce unnecessary financial stress.

Example: Imagine someone who doesn't budget, they frequently run out of money before the end of the month, unsure of where their paycheck went. Now compare that to someone who takes time to create a simple budget, allocating money for rent, groceries, savings, and personal expenses. This individual feels more in control, avoids last-minute stress, and can even plan for future goals like a vacation or debt repayment.

2. Saving for Emergencies

An emergency fund acts as a financial safety net, providing peace of mind when unexpected expenses arise. Whether it's a car repair, medical bill, or temporary income loss, having savings ensures that life's surprises don't derail your financial stability.

Example: A student sets aside just $20 from each paycheck and gradually builds a $500 emergency fund, which later helps cover an unexpected laptop repair without resorting to credit cards. Now imagine saving $100, $200 or more a month. Over time, this habit builds a larger fund that could cover months of living expenses in case of a job loss, providing long-term security and reducing financial stress.

3. Differentiating Needs vs. Wants

Understanding the difference between needs and wants is key to financial resilience. Needs are essential expenses, such as housing, food, and healthcare, while wants are discretionary items that would be nice to have but are not essential for survival. Prioritizing needs over wants helps you make smarter financial choices and avoid unnecessary debt.

Example: Imagine someone who spends just $8.00 a day on buying a specialty coffee drink five times a week. That's $40 per week, or about $160 per month—and over $1,920 a year! Now consider this: for the cost of just one month of those coffee shop drinks, they could purchase a decent coffee maker and premium coffee beans to brew at home, saving hundreds of dollars annually. By recognizing this as a "want," they can redirect their spending toward financial goals, like paying down debt or building an emergency fund, while still enjoying great coffee.

4. Long-Term Planning

Long-term financial planning helps you prepare for major life milestones, such as buying a home, starting a business, or retiring comfortably. By taking individual responsibility for your financial future, you create independence rather than dependence on external factors or others. Regular contributions to savings or investments allow you to secure your future while maintaining financial control.

Example: A young professional sets up automatic contributions to a retirement account, steadily building wealth. Over time, their consistent effort means they'll have financial independence in retirement, avoiding dependence on others or solely on government programs.

5. Paying Off Credit Card Debt

Credit card debt is a significant source of financial stress for many people but paying it off is a powerful step toward financial wellness. There are a few different strategies for tackling debt, such as paying off the card with the highest interest rate first (the avalanche method) or starting with the smallest balances to build momentum (the snowball method). As you pay down debt, you free up resources to focus on savings and long-term goals.

Example: Someone with multiple credit card balances chooses to use the avalanche method, prioritizing the card with the highest interest rate while making minimum payments on the others. Over time, this approach reduces their total interest payments and accelerates their journey to becoming debt-free. By combining this strategy with a budget, they regain financial control and reduce stress.

Practical Strategies for Financial Resilience

Financial resilience is the ability to adapt to financial changes, recover from setbacks, and plan for the future with confidence. It's not just about earning more, it's about managing what you have wisely. Whether you're saving for emergencies, paying off debt, or budgeting for long-term goals, building financial resilience reduces stress and creates a sense of stability that ripples across all areas of wellness.

1. Track Your Expenses

Understanding where your money goes is the first step to financial resilience.

- **Strategy**: Use a notebook, budgeting app, or spreadsheet to record all expenses for one month. Break them into categories like "essentials" (rent, groceries) and "discretionary" (entertainment, dining out).
  Example: A college student tracks their spending and realizes they're spending $100 a month on coffee. They redirect half of that toward savings instead.
- **Why It Works**: Tracking expenses reveals spending patterns, helping you identify areas to cut back and free up funds for priorities.

2. Start Small with Savings

Savings act as a buffer against financial emergencies and a stepping stone toward larger goals.

- **Strategy**: Begin with a manageable amount, like saving $10 a week, and increase it gradually. Automate savings to ensure consistency.

Example: An hourly wage worker opens a savings account and sets up an automatic transfer of $20 from each paycheck. Over a year, this adds up to over $500 in savings.

- **Why It Works**: Starting small makes saving feel achievable, and consistency builds financial security over time.

3. Focus on Priorities

Differentiating between needs and wants is crucial for making better financial decisions.

- **Strategy**: Evaluate purchases by asking, *"Is this a need or a want?"* Redirect funds from wants to savings or debt repayment.
  Example: Someone spending $8 on coffee five times a week ($160 per month) decides to invest in a quality coffee maker at home. They save hundreds of dollars annually while still enjoying their favorite drink.
- **Why It Works**: Prioritizing needs over wants frees up resources for essential expenses and long-term financial goals.

4. Pay Off Credit Card Debt

Carrying high-interest debt can erode financial resilience.

- **Strategy**: Use techniques like the snowball method (paying off smallest debts first) or the avalanche method (tackling highest-interest debts first).
  Example: An entrepreneur with $5,000 in credit card debt focuses on paying off the card with the highest interest rate first. By using the avalanche method and

redirecting discretionary spending to debt repayment, they reduce interest payments and pay off the debt faster.

- **Why It Works**: Paying off debt reduces financial strain, boosts credit scores, and frees up income for savings and investments.

5. Build an Emergency Fund

An emergency fund creates financial stability during unexpected events, such as medical bills or job loss.

- **Strategy**: Start by saving one month's worth of essential expenses, then aim for three to six months' worth. **Example**: A single parent sets aside $50 from each paycheck into a high-yield savings account. Over time, this provides a safety net for unplanned expenses.
- **Why It Works**: An emergency fund reduces the stress of financial uncertainty, allowing you to handle setbacks with confidence.

6. Educate Yourself

Understanding personal finance empowers you to make smarter decisions.

- **Strategy**: Take online courses, read books, or consult with a financial advisor to expand your knowledge. **Example**: An entrepreneur struggling to budget attends a free webinar on small business finances and learns strategies to manage cash flow more effectively.
- **Why It Works**: Financial literacy builds confidence and helps you avoid common pitfalls, like overspending or inadequate planning.

Even with the best strategies, building Financial Resilience isn't without its hurdles. These challenges often come in two forms: internal habits that hold you back and external pressures that feel out of your control. The good news? Recognizing these barriers is the first step toward overcoming them.

Obstacles to Building Financial Wellness

Financial wellness is a journey, and like any journey, it comes with its share of roadblocks. Whether it's the weight of old habits or unexpected external pressures, these challenges don't have to stop your progress. By identifying them early, you can transform obstacles into stepping stones toward financial stability and resilience.

Internal Obstacles

Impulse Spending

The tendency to buy things on a whim can derail financial goals and lead to regret.

- **Red Flag:** Regularly making unplanned purchases that strain your budget.
- **How to Overcome It:**
  - ➤ Create a 24-hour rule: Pause before making non-essential purchases to evaluate whether you truly need the item.
  - ➤ Track spending to identify patterns and triggers for impulsive behavior.
  - ➤ Establish a monthly "fun fund" for discretionary purchases, keeping spending under control.

Lack of Financial Knowledge

Limited understanding of budgeting, saving, or investing can make managing money feel daunting.

- **Insight Tip:** Financial literacy is a skill you can build over time—no one is born knowing it all.
- **How to Overcome It:**
    - ➤ Start with accessible resources, like online tutorials, books, or community workshops.
    - ➤ Focus on one topic at a time, such as creating a budget or understanding credit scores.
    - ➤ Consult with a financial advisor or mentor for personalized guidance.

Fear of Financial Planning

Avoiding financial planning due to anxiety or fear of failure can create long-term instability.

- **Mindset Tip:** Facing your finances head-on is the first step to gaining control and reducing stress.
- **How to Overcome It:**
    - ➤ Break financial planning into small, manageable tasks, like reviewing one bank statement at a time.
    - ➤ Set clear, achievable goals to provide direction and motivation.
    - ➤ Celebrate progress, no matter how small, to reinforce positive habits.

External Obstacles

Unpredictable Expenses

Unexpected costs, such as medical bills or car repairs, can strain even the most well-planned budget.

- **Quick Fix:** Building an emergency fund can provide a financial safety net.
- **How to Overcome It:**
    - ➢ Start saving small amounts regularly. Even $10 a week can add up over time.
    - ➢ Prioritize building an emergency fund with three to six months' worth of essential expenses.
    - ➢ Explore insurance options to mitigate financial risks from unexpected events.

Low or Irregular Income

Living paycheck-to-paycheck or experiencing fluctuating income can make it difficult to save or budget effectively.

- **Efficiency Tip:** Stability doesn't have to mean a large income; it's about managing what you have wisely.
- **How to Overcome It:**
    - ➢ Focus on budgeting based on your lowest monthly income to prepare for leaner months.
    - ➢ Seek supplemental income opportunities, such as freelancing or part-time work, to boost earnings.

> ➤ Automate savings during high-income periods to prepare for fluctuations.

Social Pressures

Feeling the need to "keep up" with others' spending habits can lead to financial strain.

- **Resolution Idea:** Align your spending with your values, not societal expectations.
- **How to Overcome It:**
  - ➤ Politely decline expensive outings and suggest affordable alternatives.
  - ➤ Remind yourself that financial wellness is about long-term goals, not short-term appearances.
  - ➤ Surround yourself with financially responsible individuals who support your goals.

A Thought on Financial Wellness Challenges

Financial challenges can feel overwhelming, but they're also some of the most solvable with the right strategies. Resilience in this area means addressing obstacles like debt, budgeting, or saving with intention and consistency. Progress in financial wellness isn't about perfectionism, it's about taking small, meaningful steps toward stability and peace of mind. By managing your finances effectively, you can create a sense of control, confidence, and long-term growth for your financial future.

Reflection Activity: What's Next?

Take a moment to reflect and ask yourself:

- *What's one financial wellness obstacle I'm ready to tackle?*

- *Which solution feels most realistic to implement this week?*

Write down your plan and commit to trying it.

Progress begins with small, intentional steps!

With obstacles and strategies for financial resilience in mind, let's reflect on how financial well-being connects to your overall balance. Let's examine the broader impact of financial wellness and how managing your resources wisely can ripple across all areas of wellness.

The Broader Impact of Financial Resilience on the other Areas of Wellness

Financial resilience isn't just about money, it's about creating stability and reducing stress. Its broader impact includes:

- **Physical Wellness**: Financial security allows you to invest in healthy food, exercise, and medical care.
- **Intellectual Wellness**: Learning financial literacy builds confidence in navigating financial challenges and opportunities.
- **Emotional Wellness**: Managing your finances reduces stress and anxiety, creating a sense of control over your life.
- **Occupational Wellness**: Financial stability empowers you to make career decisions based on fulfillment rather than necessity.
- **Social Wellness**: Financial stability fosters healthier relationships by reducing stress and encouraging shared financial goals.
- **Spiritual Wellness**: Financial security can provide the freedom to explore personal values and pursue meaningful experiences.
- **Environmental Wellness**: Managing finances helps you maintain a comfortable, well-organized living space.

Financial Wellness Scenario

Alex, the entrepreneur from earlier, realizes that while his e-commerce business is growing, his personal finances have been neglected. Expenses are scattered across multiple credit cards, his savings account is empty, and despite increasing revenue, cash flow feels perpetually tight. Each month, Alex feels anxious about making ends meet, especially during slower periods in his business. The weight of these financial struggles adds to his overall stress, leaving him feeling overwhelmed and stuck.

Determined to regain control, Alex starts by tracking his expenses. He downloads a budgeting app to categorize both personal and business spending. Within weeks, Alex identifies areas where he's overspending, like frequent takeout meals and unused business subscriptions. Armed with this knowledge, he begins cutting back on unnecessary expenses, creating more breathing room in his budget.

Next, Alex establishes a habit of saving small amounts from both his personal and business income. He sets up an automatic transfer of $50 a week into a savings account, creating an emergency fund that brings him a newfound sense of security. Knowing he has a financial cushion gives Alex the confidence to face unexpected challenges, like equipment repairs or a dip in sales.

Recognizing the burden of his credit card debt, Alex adopts the avalanche method to tackle high-interest accounts first. He redirects the money saved from cutting non-essential expenses toward his debt payments. Progress is slow but steady, and as his balances decrease, Alex feels a growing sense of accomplishment and control over his financial future.

Alex doesn't stop there. He commits to building his financial knowledge by attending workshops on small business finances and consulting with a mentor to improve his budgeting and cash flow strategies. These efforts not only help him manage his personal finances but also provide him with tools to optimize his business operations. Over time, Alex becomes more proactive and less reactive in his financial decision-making.

The changes ripple outward. As Alex's financial resilience strengthens, he notices he's less stressed and more focused on growing his business. He feels more confident in making financial decisions, both personally and professionally, and is better prepared to handle slow sales months without panic. On a personal level, the relief from financial strain allows Alex to show up more fully in his relationships, free from the cloud of worry that once followed him.

Had Alex neglected these efforts, the stress of mounting debt and poor financial management might have jeopardized both his business and personal well-being. By embracing financial resilience, Alex not only gains a sense of security and control but also builds habits that support his overall success and peace of mind.

Financial Wellness
Conclusion and Reflection Activity

Financial resilience isn't about earning the most or saving every penny—it's about building habits that give you confidence, control, and peace of mind. When you take control of your finances, you reduce stress, improve your emotional well-being, and free up resources to invest in your health, education, and relationships.

Take a moment to reflect on your financial habits and ask yourself:

- *Do I have a clear understanding of my income and expenses?*
- *Do I have credit card balances? What interest am I paying? Go back and review how to lower that debt. Map out a strategy to reduce and pay off those cards.*
- *What's one small step I can take today to improve my financial resilience, such as starting a budget or setting up a savings account?*

Examples to Get Started:

- If you're not sure where your money is going, track your expenses for one month using a notebook, spreadsheet, or app.
- If you have credit card balances, focus on paying off the card with the highest interest rate first, or use the snowball method to tackle smaller balances first for quick wins.
- If you're looking to start saving, set up an automatic transfer of even a small amount—like $10 per week—into a dedicated savings account.

Reflection Activity:

Write down one financial goal to focus on this week. Break it into manageable steps and track your progress. For example:

- *Goal*: Save $50 this week.
- *Steps*: Skip eating out twice, cancel a subscription you no longer use, and sell an item you no longer need.

Always Remember:

Financial resilience doesn't just improve your bank account, it reduces stress, increases confidence, and creates opportunities for growth in every area of life. With greater financial stability, you'll have more freedom to invest in the things that truly matter, from personal growth to meaningful experiences with loved ones.

Every step you take toward financial resilience, no matter how small, brings you closer to a more secure and balanced life. Celebrate your progress—it's an investment in your future, and it's a journey worth taking.

Disclaimer: *The strategies in this section are designed to help you build financial resilience and improve your overall well-being. However, they are not a substitute for personalized financial advice. If you're facing complex financial challenges, consult a qualified financial advisor or planner for tailored guidance.*

Occupational Wellness

Understanding
Occupational Wellness and Resilience

Occupational wellness is about finding purpose, fulfillment, and balance in your work. It involves aligning your career with your values, managing workplace stress, and maintaining a healthy work-life balance. Occupational wellness is not just about achieving professional success—it's about creating a career that supports your overall well-being.

Your occupational wellness influences your satisfaction, productivity, and ability to grow professionally. When you feel fulfilled in your work, you're more motivated, focused, and resilient in handling challenges. Occupational wellness helps you thrive, whether you're managing a team, running a business, or pursuing a creative passion.

Building occupational resilience equips you to adapt to changes in the workplace, recover from setbacks, and maintain motivation in demanding situations. It allows you to approach work challenges with confidence and create a career that aligns with your goals and well-being.

This chapter will provide strategies to enhance occupational wellness and resilience. You'll learn how to balance work and personal priorities, manage workplace stress, and find meaning in your career.

The Core Components of Occupational Resilience

1. Work-Life Balance

Work-life balance is essential for occupational wellness. It involves creating boundaries between your professional responsibilities and personal life to protect your well-being. A balanced approach prevents burnout, enhances productivity, and ensures time for rest and meaningful connections outside of work.

Example: An hourly wage worker who schedules their shifts thoughtfully, ensuring they have time for family, hobbies, or rest, finds they can approach their job with more energy and focus. They also communicate clearly with their manager about availability, creating a healthy balance without jeopardizing their employment. Similarly, an entrepreneur who schedules personal time to disconnect from work avoids burnout and maintains creativity.

2. Adaptability to Change

The ability to adapt to changes in the workplace is a cornerstone of occupational resilience. Whether it's adjusting to new technologies, evolving job roles, or shifts in the market, being flexible ensures you can handle challenges with confidence and grow in your career.

Example: A professional who learns to use a new project management software embraces the opportunity to grow their skills, making them a more valuable team member. For someone between jobs, adaptability might mean learning a new trade to align with shifting industry demands.

3. Career Development

Career development is the ongoing process of improving your skills, knowledge, and qualifications to advance in your chosen field. It empowers you to take control of your career trajectory and create opportunities for growth, no matter where your starting point is at.

Example: An individual working an entry-level job enrolls in online certification courses to build the qualifications needed for a promotion. For an entrepreneur, career development might mean attending industry conferences to stay ahead of trends and network with potential collaborators.

4. Stress Management

Managing workplace stress is critical for occupational wellness. Stress can arise from tight deadlines, workplace conflicts, or overwhelming workloads, and learning how to cope effectively ensures that you maintain both productivity and mental health.

Example: A teacher under pressure from grading deadlines practices time-blocking, dedicating specific periods to tasks and taking short breaks to stay refreshed. An entrepreneur dealing with fluctuating client demands uses mindfulness techniques to stay focused and calm under pressure. A student learns that physical activity is much better than abusive behaviors that seem fun at the time.

5. Building and Refining Your Resume

Your resume is more than just a list of accomplishments, it's a reflection of your skills, experiences, and potential. Whether you're actively job searching, seeking a promotion, or attracting clients as an entrepreneur, a strong resume ensures you stand out and showcases your unique value.

Example: A job seeker who tailors their resume for each role highlights their most relevant skills and experiences, increasing their chances of landing interviews. For a professional, keeping their resume updated allows them to be prepared for unexpected opportunities. An entrepreneur might create a portfolio-style resume that demonstrates their achievements and capabilities to potential investors or clients.

Practical Strategies for Improving Occupational Resilience

Occupational resilience is your ability to navigate the demands, pressures, and challenges of work while maintaining your well-being. Whether you're an hourly worker, a professional climbing the career ladder, an entrepreneur managing a business, or a student preparing for your future, occupational resilience allows you to adapt, grow, and thrive in your chosen field. By cultivating resilience, you can avoid burnout, improve job satisfaction, and create a healthier balance between your work and personal life.

1. Set Boundaries

Clear boundaries between work and personal life protect your well-being and prevent burnout.

- **Strategy**: Define your work hours and communicate them clearly to colleagues, supervisors, or clients. Avoid checking emails or taking work calls outside of these hours.
  Example: A professional sets a rule to stop checking emails after 6 p.m. and uses that time for family or personal activities.
- **Why It Works**: Boundaries create space for rest, recovery, and personal fulfillment, ensuring you can show up fully during work hours.

2. Invest in Growth

Continuously developing your skills and knowledge increases confidence and adaptability.

- **Strategy**: Take courses, attend workshops, or seek mentorship to advance in your field.
  Example: An entrepreneur struggling with marketing takes an online course in digital advertising, which boosts their ability to attract customers.
- **Why It Works**: Investing in your growth helps you stay competitive, build confidence, and adapt to changes in your industry or role.

3. Practice Self-Care

Maintaining mental and physical health ensures you have the energy and focus needed to perform well at work.

- **Strategy**: Prioritize habits like exercise, adequate sleep, and taking regular breaks during the workday.
  Example: An hourly worker schedules a 10-minute stretch break every two hours to reduce fatigue and improve focus.
- **Why It Works**: Self-care replenishes your energy and prevents the physical and emotional exhaustion that can derail occupational resilience.

4. Embrace Adaptability

Change is inevitable in any workplace. Learning to adapt fosters resilience and reduces stress.

- **Strategy**: When facing unexpected changes, focus on what you can control and find ways to adjust.
  Example: A manager handles a sudden team restructuring by redefining roles and seeking input from team members to maintain morale.
- **Why It Works**: Adaptability allows you to navigate uncertainty with confidence and maintain productivity under shifting circumstances.

5. Build a Supportive Network

Professional relationships can provide encouragement, guidance, and new opportunities.

- **Strategy**: Cultivate connections with colleagues, mentors, and industry peers through networking events or regular check-ins.
  Example: A student nearing graduation joins a professional association to connect with potential mentors and learn about job opportunities.
- **Why It Works**: A strong network offers emotional and professional support, helping you overcome challenges and discover new paths.

6. Reflect and Reassess

Regularly evaluating your career goals ensures your work aligns with your values and aspirations.

- **Strategy**: Set aside time to reflect on your current role, achievements, and areas for improvement. Adjust your goals or career path as needed.
  Example: A mid-career professional realizes they feel unfulfilled in their current role and starts exploring opportunities in a field they're passionate about.
- **Why It Works**: Reflection helps you stay motivated and aligned with your personal and professional goals, enhancing job satisfaction.

Occupational Resilience is an essential part of maintaining balance and fulfillment in your professional life. However, even the best strategies can encounter roadblocks. These challenges often fall into two categories: internal struggles, such as burnout or lack of focus, and external circumstances, like workplace changes or demanding schedules. Recognizing these barriers is the first step to overcoming them and thriving in your career.

Obstacles to Building Occupational Wellness

Achieving occupational wellness often requires navigating a variety of challenges, both internal and external. These obstacles can affect job satisfaction, work-life balance, and professional growth. Understanding and addressing these hurdles can empower you to create a more fulfilling and resilient career path.

Internal Obstacles

Burnout

Prolonged stress, overwork, or lack of fulfillment can lead to emotional exhaustion and decreased productivity.

- **Red Flag:** Feeling consistently drained, cynical, or unmotivated about your work.
- **How to Overcome It:**
  - Set boundaries to protect your personal time, such as not checking emails after work hours.
  - Incorporate self-care practices, like exercise or relaxation techniques, into your routine to recharge.
  - Prioritize tasks by identifying what's urgent and important, delegating or postponing less critical tasks.

Lack of Career Direction

Uncertainty about long-term goals or a sense of stagnation can diminish engagement and satisfaction.

- **Insight Tip:** Your career path doesn't have to be linear. Exploration is part of growth.
- **How to Overcome It:**
  - ➢ Reflect on your strengths, interests, and values to identify what truly matters to you.
  - ➢ Set small, actionable career goals, such as learning a new skill or exploring a different role within your field.
  - ➢ Seek mentorship or career counseling to gain clarity and direction.

Imposter Syndrome

Doubting your abilities or feeling unqualified can hinder confidence and career progression.

- **Mindset Tip:** Remember, growth often happens outside your comfort zone.
- **How to Overcome It:**
  - ➢ Keep a record of your accomplishments and positive feedback to remind yourself of your value.
  - ➢ Challenge negative self-talk by focusing on facts rather than fears.
  - ➢ Embrace a growth mindset, viewing challenges as opportunities to learn and improve.

External Obstacles

Toxic Work Environment

Unsupportive colleagues, poor management, or an unhealthy company culture can negatively impact well-being.

- **Quick Fix:** Focus on what you can control while exploring long-term solutions.
- **How to Overcome It:**
  - ➤ Document instances of inappropriate behavior or conflicts to address them professionally if needed.
  - ➤ Establish boundaries to protect your emotional energy, such as limiting interactions with negative colleagues.
  - ➤ Consider exploring new job opportunities if the environment becomes untenable.

Limited Opportunities for Growth

Feeling stuck in a role without prospects for advancement can lead to dissatisfaction and frustration.

- **Efficiency Tip:** Growth isn't always about promotions—it's about learning and contributing meaningfully.
- **How to Overcome It:**
  - ➤ Seek out additional responsibilities or projects that align with your interests and goals.

- ➢ Invest in professional development, such as taking courses, attending workshops, or pursuing certifications.
- ➢ Network within and outside your organization to discover new opportunities.

Work-Life Imbalance

Excessive work demands can encroach on personal time, leading to stress and a decreased quality of life.

- **Resolution Idea:** A balanced schedule supports both productivity and well-being.
- **How to Overcome It:**
  - ➢ Schedule personal activities like you would work tasks to ensure they're prioritized.
  - ➢ Learn to say "no" to additional responsibilities that would compromise your balance.
  - ➢ Communicate your boundaries clearly to colleagues and supervisors.

A Thought on Occupational Wellness Challenges

Challenges in the workplace are inevitable—whether it's managing workloads, adapting to change, or navigating workplace dynamics. Building occupational resilience means approaching these obstacles with intentional strategies to create a work life that supports your goals and overall well-being. It's not just about thriving in your job; it's about finding harmony between work and life. By viewing challenges as opportunities to grow your skills and confidence, you can stay adaptable, maintain balance, and foster a fulfilling and resilient career.

Reflection Activity: What's Next?

Take a moment to reflect and ask yourself:

- *What's one occupational wellness obstacle I'm ready to tackle?*

- *Which solution feels most realistic to implement this week?*

Write down your plan and commit to trying it.

Small, consistent changes can transform your work experience!

Having explored the challenges and strategies for occupational resilience, let's reflect on how finding balance and purpose at work can influence your broader well-being. Let's examine the ripple effect of occupational wellness and how it supports all eight areas of resilience.

The Broader Impact of Occupational Resilience on the other Areas of Wellness

Occupational resilience allows you to adapt to workplace challenges while maintaining balance in your life. Its ripple effect strengthens:

- **Physical Wellness**: A healthy work-life balance supports better sleep, nutrition, and physical activity.
- **Intellectual Wellness**: Developing new skills and seeking professional growth keeps your mind engaged and adaptable.
- **Emotional Wellness**: Setting boundaries and finding meaning in your work reduces stress and improves overall mental health.
- **Financial Wellness**: Job satisfaction and career stability provide the income needed to support other areas of wellness.
- **Social Wellness**: Positive workplace relationships foster collaboration and a sense of belonging.
- **Spiritual Wellness**: Aligning your work with your values gives you a sense of purpose and fulfillment.
- **Environmental Wellness**: A well-organized workspace reduces stress and boosts productivity.

Occupational Wellness Scenario

As Alex's e-commerce business grows, the demands of managing inventory, marketing, and customer service pile up. He often finds himself working late into the night, skipping meals, and neglecting personal time. The constant pressure starts to take a toll—Alex's productivity declines, he feels increasingly overwhelmed, and the business's growth begins to stall. The lack of balance also affects Alex's personal relationships, as he becomes more irritable and less present with loved ones.

Recognizing that his current approach is unsustainable, Alex decides to prioritize building occupational resilience. The first step is setting boundaries. Alex establishes clear work hours from 9 a.m. to 6 p.m., dedicating his evenings to rest, family, and personal pursuits. At first, the shift feels difficult, but over time, Alex notices that the structure allows him to recharge, and approach work with renewed focus and energy.

Next, Alex invests in professional growth. He attends workshops on time management and learns techniques for delegating responsibilities. With newfound confidence, Alex hires a small team to help with customer service and inventory management. This reduces his workload and allows him to focus on higher-level strategies that drive the business forward.

Incorporating self-care into his routine becomes another priority for Alex. He starts taking short walks during lunch breaks and ensures he gets a full night's sleep. These small changes improve his energy levels and clarity, helping him stay productive throughout the day. When a sudden drop in sales occurs due to a competitor's aggressive marketing campaign, Alex leans into adaptability. Drawing on insights gained from a network of fellow entrepreneurs, he quickly revamps his marketing strategy, launching a targeted campaign that revitalizes sales.

Reflecting on his goals, Alex takes a step back to assess the bigger picture. He realizes that expanding into new markets aligns with his long-term aspirations and develops a plan to diversify his offerings. By aligning his work with his broader vision, Alex not only finds satisfaction in his accomplishments but also creates a more sustainable path for the business.

Without these changes, Alex risked burnout, stagnation, and even jeopardizing his relationships. By building occupational resilience, Alex finds balance, satisfaction, and a renewed sense of purpose in both his work and personal life. He learns that success isn't about working harder but about working smarter and prioritizing what truly matters.

Occupational Wellness
Conclusion and Reflection Activity

Occupational resilience isn't just about navigating challenges, it's about thriving in your career while maintaining balance and fulfillment in your life. By building resilience in this area, you empower yourself to adapt to workplace changes, manage stress, and pursue growth opportunities with confidence.

Take a moment to reflect on your workplace habits and ask yourself:

- *How do I currently respond to workplace challenges or changes?*
- *What's one way I could build occupational resilience, such as setting boundaries, learning a new skill, or updating my resume?*
- *Am I satisfied with my work-life balance? If not, what's one small change I could make to improve it?*

Examples to Get Started:

- If you're feeling overwhelmed at work, consider setting clear boundaries, such as committing to leaving the office on time twice a week or avoiding work emails after hours.
- If you've been in the same role for years, explore an online course or workshop to learn a new skill and expand your career options.
- If your resume hasn't been updated in years, take an hour this week to refresh it with your most recent accomplishments.

Reflection Activity:

Write down one occupational resilience strategy to focus on this week. Track your progress by reflecting on these questions:

- *How did this strategy improve my workplace experience?*

- *Did it reduce stress or enhance my work-life balance?*

- *What's the next step I can take to build on this success?*

Always Remember:

Occupational resilience doesn't just benefit your career—it enhances your overall well-being. By managing workplace stress and pursuing growth opportunities, you improve your emotional resilience, build confidence, and create a greater sense of control over your life.

Every small step you take toward occupational resilience brings you closer to a career that aligns with your goals and values. Celebrate your progress and trust in your ability to adapt, grow, and thrive.

Disclaimer: *The strategies in this section are designed to help you build occupational resilience and improve workplace satisfaction. However, they are not a substitute for professional career counseling or human resources guidance. If you're facing complex workplace challenges, consult a qualified professional for personalized advice.*

Social Wellness

Understanding
Social Wellness and Resilience

Social wellness is about creating and maintaining strong, meaningful connections with others. It involves effective communication, empathy, and the ability to build supportive relationships that enrich your life. Social wellness isn't just about the number of relationships you have—it's about the quality of those connections.

In your daily life, social wellness provides emotional support, reduces stress, and creates a sense of belonging. Whether it's with family, friends, colleagues, or community members, maintaining strong relationships helps you navigate life's challenges with greater ease and confidence.

Building social resilience strengthens your ability to adapt to changes in relationships, resolve conflicts, and maintain meaningful connections even during difficult times. It allows you to grow your support network and foster relationships that uplift and empower you.

This chapter will explore strategies to enhance social wellness and resilience. You'll learn how to communicate effectively, navigate social challenges, and build a network of strong, supportive relationships.

The Core Components of Social Resilience

1. Building Supportive Relationships

Strong relationships are the foundation of social wellness. These are connections with people who provide emotional support, encouragement, and a sense of belonging. Supportive relationships help you navigate challenges and celebrate successes, fostering resilience and well-being. However, not all relationships are truly supportive. Be cautious of individuals, such as narcissists or those who exploit others' vulnerabilities, under the guise of friendship.

Example: Someone who regularly spends time with a close group of friends feels more emotionally grounded and confident during tough times because they have people to lean on for advice, laughter, or simply a listening ear. By reflecting on the nature of their friendships, they ensure these relationships are mutual and uplifting.

2. Effective Communication

Communication is the key to maintaining healthy relationships. This includes not only expressing yourself clearly but also listening actively, empathizing with others, and responding in a way that nurtures connection. Effective communication strengthens bonds, resolves conflicts, and ensures your needs are understood and respected.

Example: A coworker who feels overwhelmed with a project communicates their concerns honestly with their manager and provides a proposed solution, such as extending a deadline or delegating tasks. By addressing the issue constructively and showing initiative, they strengthen the trust and rapport in their professional relationship. Similarly, a student who actively participates in group discussions builds collaborative skills while earning respect from peers and instructors.

3. Conflict Resolution

No relationship is without challenges, but the ability to address and resolve conflicts constructively is essential for social resilience. Conflict resolution involves staying calm, listening to all perspectives, and working toward a solution that respects everyone involved. This skill can be especially valuable in uncomfortable decision-making situations, such as joint purchases or shared responsibilities.

Example: Two friends planning a group trip disagree on the budget. Instead of letting tensions build, they discuss their priorities and agree on compromises—splitting accommodations to save costs or choosing fewer activities to balance expenses. By working through the discomfort, they maintain their friendship while making a responsible decision.

4. Expanding Your Network

Your social network isn't limited to close friends and family, it also includes acquaintances, colleagues, and community members. Expanding your network introduces you to new perspectives, opportunities, and support systems. It's about cultivating meaningful connections beyond your inner circle, both locally and globally, using tools like social media platforms to reach across borders and industries.

Example: A student attends a career fair, meeting professionals in their field who provide guidance and mentorship, giving them valuable insights as they prepare to enter the workforce. Similarly, a professional who participates in LinkedIn discussions or attends virtual industry webinars connects with peers from around the world, gaining fresh perspectives and access to global opportunities. An entrepreneur who shares their work on social platforms builds connections with clients or collaborators from different countries, broadening their reach and influence.

5. Understanding the Impact of Social Media

Social media plays a significant role in modern relationships, influencing how we connect and communicate. While it can be a powerful tool for staying in touch, sharing ideas, and building communities, it can also become a source of fake news, propaganda, selfish trolls, and toxic comparisons. Building social resilience means using social media intentionally, verifying information, and focusing on genuine interactions that enhance your well-being.

Example: An entrepreneur notices their feed is flooded with posts promoting unrealistic success stories, leading to frustration and self-doubt. By unfollowing accounts that fuel negativity and verifying news through trusted sources, they curate a healthier online space. Similarly, a student becomes more aware of fake news and learns to question and verify information before sharing or reacting, fostering a more thoughtful digital presence.

Practical Strategies for Enhancing Social Resilience

Social resilience is the ability to build, maintain, and adapt relationships in the face of challenges. It's about fostering meaningful connections, navigating conflict with grace, and expanding your social network to support personal and professional growth. Whether you're an entrepreneur, professional, student, or parent, social resilience helps you thrive by creating a strong web of relationships that provide encouragement, perspective, and belonging.

1. Reach Out Regularly

Consistent communication strengthens relationships and fosters emotional support.

- **Strategy**: Set reminders to reach out to loved ones through calls, texts, or visits, even when life gets busy. **Example**: A busy entrepreneur dedicates Sunday evenings to calling a family member or catching up with an old friend.
- **Why It Works**: Regular contact keeps relationships alive, showing others you value and care for them.

2. Practice Active Listening

Active listening helps you connect with others by showing that you value their perspective.

- **Strategy**: During conversations, focus fully on the speaker, ask follow-up questions, and summarize what they've said to confirm understanding.
  Example: A coworker shares their challenges with a project, and you respond by saying, *"It sounds like you're feeling stuck because of limited resources. Is that right?"*
- **Why It Works**: Active listening builds trust, strengthens bonds, and improves communication in all types of relationships.

3. Strengthen Weak Ties

Reconnecting with acquaintances and colleagues can open doors to new opportunities and broaden your network.

- **Strategy**: Send a friendly email or direct message to someone you haven't spoken to in a while.
  Example: A professional reaches out to a former coworker to ask about job opportunities, leading to a new collaboration.
- **Why It Works**: Weak ties often serve as valuable connections for resources, advice, or opportunities that your close network may not provide.

4. Set Boundaries in Relationships

Healthy boundaries protect your emotional energy and prevent toxic interactions.

- **Strategy**: Be clear about what you're comfortable with and communicate those limits kindly but firmly. **Example**: A student overwhelmed with group project demands sets a boundary by agreeing to specific tasks but declining extra work outside their role.
- **Why It Works**: Boundaries maintain balance and reduce stress in relationships, allowing you to focus on meaningful connections.

5. Seek Diversity in Your Network

Engaging with people from different backgrounds broadens your perspective and fosters empathy.

- **Strategy**: Attend events, join groups, or participate in discussions that bring together diverse individuals. **Example**: An entrepreneur attends a local meetup focused on sustainability and gains new ideas for making their business eco-friendly.
- **Why It Works**: A diverse network exposes you to new ideas, challenges assumptions, and strengthens your ability to navigate complex social dynamics.

Social Resilience is critical to building strong, meaningful relationships and navigating the challenges of social dynamics. Even with the best strategies, obstacles can arise, such as internal struggles with communication or external pressures from difficult relationships. Recognizing these barriers is a vital step toward creating a supportive social network and enhancing your connections.

Obstacles to Building Social Wellness

Social wellness plays a crucial role in overall well-being, but it can be challenged by both internal and external obstacles. Identifying these hurdles is the first step toward fostering meaningful relationships and building a strong support network. This section explores common challenges and actionable strategies to overcome them.

Internal Obstacles

Fear of Vulnerability

Feeling hesitant to open up or share emotions can hinder deep connections with others.

- **Red Flag:** Avoiding meaningful conversations or keeping relationships at a surface level out of fear of judgment or rejection.
- **How to Overcome It:**
  - ➢ Start small by sharing a personal story or thought with someone you trust.
  - ➢ Practice active listening to create a safe space for others, which often encourages reciprocal vulnerability.
  - ➢ Remind yourself that building trust takes time, and vulnerability is a strength, not a weakness.

Lack of Confidence

Feeling unsure about social skills or doubting your value in relationships can prevent you from engaging with others.

- **Insight Tip:** Confidence in social settings grows with practice and positive reinforcement.
- **How to Overcome It:**
  - ➢ Attend low-pressure social events to gradually build comfort in group settings.
  - ➢ Focus on being genuinely interested in others instead of worrying about how you appear.
  - ➢ Celebrate small successes, like initiating a conversation or reconnecting with an old friend.

Overcommitment

Saying "yes" to too many social obligations can lead to exhaustion and dilute the quality of your interactions.

- **Mindset Tip:** Quality trumps quantity when it comes to meaningful relationships.
- **How to Overcome It:**
  - ➢ Prioritize relationships that energize and uplift you and politely decline others when needed.
  - ➢ Schedule time for self-care and reflection, ensuring social commitments don't overwhelm personal time.
  - ➢ Communicate your limits clearly and kindly with friends and family.

External Obstacles

Physical Distance

Being far away from loved ones can make maintaining relationships challenging.

- **Quick Fix:** Technology can bridge the gap and keep you connected.
- **How to Overcome It:**
  - ➤ Schedule regular video calls, phone calls, or virtual hangouts to stay in touch.
  - ➤ Use social media intentionally to share updates and check in with distant friends and family.
  - ➤ Plan visits or meet-ups, when possible, even if they're infrequent.

Toxic Relationships

Negative or manipulative people can drain your emotional energy and erode your confidence.

- **Efficiency Tip:** Recognizing unhealthy dynamics is the first step to protecting your well-being.
- **How to Overcome It:**
  - ➤ Set firm boundaries to minimize the impact of toxic individuals.
  - ➤ Seek support from trusted friends or counselors to navigate complex relationships.
  - ➤ Surround yourself with positive influences who encourage growth and happiness.

Social Media Overload

Constant exposure to curated content can lead to feelings of inadequacy or strain relationships.

- **Resolution Idea:** Use social media as a tool for connection, not comparison.
- **How to Overcome It:**
  - ➤ Unfollow or mute accounts that negatively impact your mental health.
  - ➤ Limit screen time and focus on in-person connections.
  - ➤ Use social media to strengthen relationships by engaging with meaningful content and reaching out to others.

A Thought on Social Wellness Challenges

Building and maintaining social wellness takes effort, but the rewards are well worth it. By addressing obstacles and focusing on authentic, supportive relationships, you create a network that nurtures your well-being and helps you thrive. Social challenges can take many forms, from strained relationships to feelings of isolation. These difficulties, while uncomfortable, offer a chance to build stronger connections and learn healthier ways to communicate. Resilience in social wellness is about showing up for yourself and others, even when it's hard.

Reflection Activity: What's Next?

Take a moment to reflect and ask yourself:

- *What's one social wellness obstacle I'm ready to tackle?*

- *Which solution feels most realistic to implement this week?*

Write down your plan and commit to trying it.

Small, intentional actions can transform your social connections and strengthen your support network!

After addressing the challenges and solutions for social resilience, let's consider how meaningful connections and support networks enhance more than just your relationships. Let's explore the broader impact of social wellness and how fostering strong connections supports overall well-being.

The Broader Impact of Social Resilience on the other Areas of Wellness

Social resilience strengthens your ability to connect, communicate, and build meaningful relationships. Its broader impact includes:

- **Physical Wellness**: Strong social connections can improve mental health, lower blood pressure, and boost immunity.
- **Intellectual Wellness**: Engaging with diverse perspectives enriches your thinking and challenges your worldview.
- **Emotional Wellness**: Supportive relationships provide emotional security and reduce feelings of loneliness or stress.
- **Financial Wellness**: Social networks can provide financial advice, resources, or opportunities.
- **Occupational Wellness**: Strong professional relationships foster collaboration, mentorship, and career growth.
- **Spiritual Wellness**: Relationships rooted in shared values can deepen your sense of purpose and connection.
- **Environmental Wellness**: A socially supportive home or community fosters a nurturing environment.

Social Wellness Scenario

As Alex's e-commerce business grows, he finds himself increasingly isolated. Long hours, constant decision-making, and the pressure to succeed have left little time for personal connections. Over time, Alex realizes his social circle has shrunk to just clients and suppliers, and even those interactions feel transactional. Without meaningful relationships to provide encouragement or fresh ideas, Alex begins to feel stressed and burned out.

Determined to rebuild his social resilience, Alex starts by reaching out regularly to friends and family. He sets a goal to make weekly calls and schedule occasional meetups, even if it's just for a quick coffee or a casual catch-up. These moments of connection provide Alex with emotional support and a renewed sense of belonging, reminding him that he's not alone in his journey.

Next, Alex begins practicing active listening during conversations with his team. By giving his employees his full attention, asking thoughtful questions, and genuinely considering their input, Alex strengthens relationships within the workplace. The shift improves team morale and fosters a spirit of collaboration, making the business run more smoothly.

Alex also decides to reconnect with former colleagues and acquaintances. One reconnection leads to a valuable partnership—an old friend introduces Alex to a new supplier, significantly cutting costs and increasing profit margins. This experience reinforces the value of maintaining and strengthening weak ties, as they often lead to unexpected opportunities.

Recognizing the importance of balance, Alex learns to set boundaries with demanding clients. Politely but firmly declining unreasonable requests helps protect his emotional energy, allowing him to maintain healthier, more productive relationships with the clients who truly align with his business values.

Finally, Alex seeks diversity in his connections by joining a local networking group that includes entrepreneurs from a variety of industries. These interactions expose Alex to fresh perspectives and innovative ideas, inspiring him to try new approaches in his business. The group also becomes a source of encouragement and camaraderie, helping Alex feel less isolated and more supported.

Without these efforts, Alex might have continued to feel disconnected and overwhelmed, potentially impacting both his emotional well-being and the success of his business. By building social resilience, Alex finds connection, support, and inspiration, enriching both his personal and professional life. His renewed social network becomes a foundation for not only achieving his goals but also enjoying the journey.

Social Wellness
Conclusion and Reflection Activity

Social resilience is the foundation of meaningful connections. It's about creating a support network that not only helps you through challenges but also amplifies your joys and successes. By nurturing your relationships, you build a sense of belonging and emotional strength that carries you through life's ups and downs.

Take a moment to reflect on your social connections and ask yourself:

- *Who supports me emotionally or practically when challenges arise?*
- *What's one step I can take to strengthen my social resilience, such as reaching out to a friend or joining a community group?*
- *Audit your social media: Are there accounts, groups, or interactions that drain my energy? What can I do to remove sources of stress and curate a more positive digital environment?*

Examples to Get Started:

- If you're feeling isolated, think of one friend or family member you haven't connected with in a while. Send them a message, call them, or make plans to meet up.
- If social media feels overwhelming, start by unfollowing accounts that don't bring you joy or value and follow groups that inspire and uplift you.
- If you've been wanting to meet new people, consider joining a community group, attending a workshop, or volunteering for a cause you're passionate about.

Reflection Activity:

Write down one action you'll take this week to strengthen your social resilience. At the end of the week, reflect on these questions:

- *How did this action make me feel?*

- *Did it strengthen my sense of connection or reduce stress?*

- *What's one more step I can take to continue building my social resilience?*

Always Remember:

Social resilience doesn't just enhance your relationships, it improves your emotional well-being, reduces stress, and supports your ability to navigate challenges in other areas of life. When you nurture your social connections, you create a ripple effect of positivity that touches every part of your wellness.

Every effort you make to nurture your social resilience builds a network of support and positivity that strengthens every aspect of your life. Celebrate the connections you've made and the new ones you're building—each one is a step toward a more fulfilling and balanced life.

Disclaimer: *The strategies in this section are designed to help you build social resilience and navigate relationships effectively. However, they are not a substitute for professional counseling or conflict resolution services. If you face significant interpersonal challenges, consider seeking guidance from a qualified therapist or mediator.*

Spiritual Wellness

Understanding
Spiritual Wellness and Resilience

Spiritual wellness is about connecting with your values, purpose, and sense of meaning in life. It involves cultivating inner peace, practicing mindfulness, and staying aligned with what truly matters to you. *Spiritual wellness doesn't require religious belief*, it's about nurturing a sense of purpose and grounding.

In your daily life, spiritual wellness provides clarity, hope, and strength during times of uncertainty. It helps you make decisions that align with your values and find balance amidst life's demands. Spiritual wellness encourages you to reflect on what's most important and live with intention.

Building spiritual resilience deepens your ability to stay grounded and hopeful, even in challenging times. It empowers you to adapt to adversity with clarity, optimism, and a sense of connection to something greater than yourself.

This chapter will guide you in cultivating spiritual wellness and resilience. Through mindfulness practices, reflection, and purposeful living, you'll gain tools to strengthen your inner peace and alignment.

Spiritual Wellness (as framed in this book) Is Not About Religion

Spiritual wellness is a universal concept that applies to people of all beliefs and backgrounds. While religion can play a role in spiritual wellness for some, this chapter focuses on practices and principles that are independent of religious affiliation. Concepts such as aligning with your values, finding purpose, and cultivating mindfulness are accessible to everyone and don't rely on adherence to any specific doctrine.

This chapter aims to provide tools that foster personal growth, inner peace, and a connection to the world around you, regardless of whether religion is part of your life. The goal is to build spiritual resilience in ways that resonate with your unique journey.

The Core Components of Spiritual Resilience

1. Connecting with Your Values

Spiritual wellness begins with understanding and aligning your actions with your core values. When you're connected to what truly matters to you—such as integrity, kindness, or growth— you gain clarity and purpose, even during life's challenges. This alignment strengthens resilience by helping you make decisions and navigate adversity with confidence.

Example: An entrepreneur considering a business partnership chooses to prioritize honesty and transparency, even if it means turning down a profitable opportunity. Similarly, a student deciding whether to speak up during a group project reflects on their values of teamwork and fairness, finding the courage to voice their concerns constructively.

2. Finding Purpose

Having a sense of purpose gives your life direction and meaning. It doesn't have to be tied to grand achievements, it can be found in the small, meaningful ways you contribute to others and the world. Purpose motivates you to keep moving forward, even when challenges arise.

Example: A stay-at-home parent finds purpose in creating a supportive environment for their family, while a teacher discovers fulfillment in helping students build confidence. Similarly, an hourly worker who volunteers at a local food bank on weekends finds purpose in giving back to their community, even beyond their daily responsibilities.

3. Practicing Mindfulness

Mindfulness is the practice of being present and fully engaged in the moment. It helps you reduce stress, improve focus, and find balance amidst the chaos of daily life. Mindfulness also deepens your connection to yourself and the world around you, enhancing your overall well-being.

Example: A busy professional sets aside time to take mindful walks during lunch breaks, appreciating the moment instead of focusing on work stress. Similarly, a student uses mindfulness techniques before exams to manage anxiety, stay calm, and approach challenges with a clear mind.

4. Attitude and Perspective

A positive attitude and a balanced perspective are powerful tools for spiritual wellness. Your attitude shapes how you approach life's challenges, while your perspective helps you see the bigger picture. Together, they allow you to focus on possibilities rather than limitations, reinforcing resilience.

Example: A student struggling with multiple deadlines chooses to focus on creating a realistic schedule and tackling one task at a time instead of feeling overwhelmed. Similarly, an employee facing criticism at work reflects on it as an opportunity to improve and grow, maintaining a constructive mindset despite initial discomfort.

5. Maintaining Hope

Hope is a powerful and practical mindset that fuels resilience. It's not about wishful thinking or ignoring challenges, it's about cultivating the confidence that you have the strength, resources, and determination to overcome obstacles. Hope is grounded in the belief that your actions can lead to meaningful progress, even in difficult circumstances. It empowers you to focus on solutions and take proactive steps toward growth and success.

Example: A professional facing layoff channels their energy into networking, acquiring new skills, and pursuing opportunities, confident that their efforts will lead to a better outcome. Similarly, a student grappling with a challenging course reflects on the strategies that have worked in the past, trusting their ability to adapt and succeed as they tackle the current challenge.

Practical Strategies for Elevating Spiritual Resilience

Spiritual resilience is the ability to find purpose, meaning, and connection in life, even during challenging times. It's not tied to any specific religion or belief system—instead, it's about understanding your core values, nurturing your sense of purpose, and staying grounded in what truly matters to you. Spiritual resilience helps you maintain hope, clarity, and balance, even when life feels uncertain or overwhelming.

Building spiritual resilience isn't about perfection or rigid practice, it's about discovering what connects you to a deeper sense of meaning and finding practices that restore your inner strength.

1. Reflect on Your Values

Understanding what truly matters to you helps create a strong foundation for decision-making and purpose.

- **Strategy**: Write down your core values and reflect on how they guide your daily actions.
  Example: A professional identifies "helping others" as a core value and chooses a volunteer opportunity that aligns with it.
- **Why It Works**: Reflecting on your values clarifies priorities and provides direction during uncertain times.

2. Practice Gratitude

Focusing on the positives in your life fosters a sense of fulfillment and connection.

- **Strategy:** Keep a gratitude journal and write down three things you're thankful for each day.
  Example: A student lists simple joys like supportive classmates, a sunny day, and completing a difficult assignment.
- **Why It Works:** Gratitude shifts your mindset, helping you find meaning and joy even in small moments.

3. Engage in Mindfulness

Mindfulness helps you connect with your inner self and quiet the mental clutter that can arise during stress.

- **Strategy:** Spend five minutes daily in quiet reflection, focusing on your breath or simply observing your thoughts.
  Example: An entrepreneur takes a short mindfulness break during a hectic day to reset and refocus.
- **Why It Works:** Mindfulness nurtures clarity, reduces stress, and deepens your connection with yourself.

4. Connect with a Community

Engaging with like-minded individuals fosters a sense of belonging and shared purpose.

- **Strategy**: Join a group or community that aligns with your values, such as a book club, volunteer organization, or mindfulness group.
  Example: A caregiver joins a local support group to share experiences and find encouragement from others facing similar challenges.
- **Why It Works**: Community provides emotional support, inspiration, and a reminder that you're not alone in your journey.

5. Explore Nature

Spending time outdoors can restore a sense of wonder and connection to something larger than yourself.

- **Strategy**: Take regular walks in natural settings, such as a park, forest, or beach, and focus on your surroundings.
  Example: An office worker spends weekends hiking in the mountains, using the quiet time to reflect on their goals and recharge.
- **Why It Works**: Nature offers a grounding experience, helping you feel more centered and connected to the world.

6. Align Actions with Values

Living in alignment with your values reinforces a sense of purpose and integrity.

- **Strategy:** Reflect on whether your actions reflect your core values and make adjustments where needed. **Example:** A professional prioritizes honesty by setting realistic expectations with clients rather than overpromising.
- **Why It Works:** When your actions align with your values, you feel more fulfilled and confident in your choices.

Spiritual Resilience plays a vital role in connecting with your values, finding meaning, and maintaining a sense of purpose. Even with the best intentions, obstacles can arise. These challenges often fall into two categories: internal struggles, such as uncertainty or lack of focus, and external pressures, like societal expectations or limited time for reflection. Recognizing these barriers is a key step to strengthening your spiritual foundation and fostering resilience.

Obstacles to Building Spiritual Wellness

Spiritual wellness involves connecting with your core values, finding purpose, and fostering a sense of meaning in life. However, internal and external challenges can arise, making it difficult to maintain a sense of spiritual balance. Identifying these barriers can help you take actionable steps toward cultivating a deeper connection to your values and purpose.

Internal Obstacles

Lack of Clarity

Feeling uncertain about your personal values or what gives your life meaning can create a sense of disconnection.

- **Red Flag:** Avoiding reflection on life's purpose or feeling lost during challenging times.
- **How to Overcome It:**
  - ➤ Spend time reflecting on your core beliefs and values. Journaling or guided meditation can help clarify what truly matters to you.
  - ➤ Try new activities, like volunteering or creative hobbies, to discover what brings you joy and fulfillment.
  - ➤ Regularly revisit and refine your values to ensure they align with your current goals and priorities.

Inconsistent Practices

Struggling to maintain consistent habits, such as mindfulness, gratitude, or reflection, can weaken your sense of purpose over time.

- **Insight Tip:** Spiritual practices thrive on routine and repetition.
- **How to Overcome It:**
  - ➢ Start small by dedicating five minutes daily to a spiritual practice, such as meditation, prayer, or gratitude journaling.
  - ➢ Set reminders or pair practices with existing habits—for instance, practicing gratitude before meals or reflecting during your morning coffee.
  - ➢ Join a group or class that focuses on mindfulness or spiritual growth to create accountability.

Self-Doubt

Doubting your ability to connect with something greater or questioning whether spiritual practices are "working" can lead to frustration.

- **Mindset Tip:** Spiritual growth is a journey, not a destination.
- **How to Overcome It:**
  - ➢ Focus on the process rather than immediate results, trusting that small efforts accumulate over time.

- ➢ Read books or listen to podcasts on spirituality for inspiration and encouragement.
- ➢ Seek out mentors, guides, or role models who can share their own experiences and provide guidance.

External Obstacles

Cultural or Social Expectations

Feeling pressure to conform to societal or cultural norms that don't align with your personal beliefs can create tension.

- **Quick Fix:** Your spiritual journey is uniquely yours—it doesn't have to match anyone else's.
- **How to Overcome It:**
  - ➢ Give yourself permission to explore spirituality in your own way, without comparing your path to others.
  - ➢ Seek communities or groups that share similar values to foster a sense of belonging.
  - ➢ Politely set boundaries with those who try to impose their spiritual views on you.

Busy Schedules

Finding time for spiritual reflection amidst work, family, and social obligations can be challenging.

- **Efficiency Tip:** Integrate spirituality into your daily routine to make it manageable.
- **How to Overcome It:**

148

➢ Incorporate moments of mindfulness or gratitude into everyday activities, like commuting, cooking, or walking.
➢ Block out small, consistent periods of time for spiritual practices, such as five minutes in the morning or before bed.
➢ Use apps or guided resources to fit mindfulness or meditation into your schedule.

Environmental Distractions

A noisy, chaotic, or cluttered environment can disrupt your ability to focus on spiritual practices.

- **Resolution Idea:** Create a calm and intentional space for reflection, even if it's just a small corner of your home.
- **How to Overcome It:**
  ➢ Declutter and organize a dedicated area for mindfulness, meditation, or journaling.
  ➢ Use calming elements like candles, plants, or soft lighting to set the tone for spiritual reflection.
  ➢ Minimize digital distractions by silencing notifications during your spiritual practices.

A Thought on Spiritual Wellness Challenges

The journey to spiritual wellness is deeply personal, and obstacles are a natural part of growth. By identifying and addressing these challenges, you create space for greater connection, meaning, and purpose in your life. Remember, the process of nurturing spiritual wellness is just as important as the outcomes.

Challenges to spiritual resilience often come in the form of feeling disconnected, lacking purpose, or facing difficult life transitions. These moments can be tough but are also opportunities to reconnect with what truly matters to you. Resilience in this area is about staying grounded and open to growth.

Reflection Activity: What's Next?

Take a moment to reflect and ask yourself:

- *What's one obstacle I'm ready to address on my spiritual journey?*

- *Which solution feels most aligned with my current needs and values?*

Write down your plan and commit to exploring it this week.

Small, meaningful actions can pave the way for profound spiritual growth and connection.

With the obstacles and strategies for spiritual resilience in mind, let's reflect on how cultivating purpose and connection can influence all areas of your life. Let's explore the broader impact of spiritual wellness and how grounding yourself in your values enhances total well-being.

The Broader Impact of Spiritual Resilience on the other Areas of Wellness

Spiritual resilience connects you to your values and purpose, fostering peace and clarity. Its impact extends to:

- **Physical Wellness**: Practices like meditation or gratitude can reduce stress and promote physical relaxation.
- **Intellectual Wellness**: Exploring spiritual philosophies encourages reflection and a deeper understanding of life's complexities.
- **Emotional Wellness**: Spirituality provides a sense of hope and grounding during life's challenges.
- **Financial Wellness**: Spiritual clarity can influence financial decisions based on priorities and values.
- **Occupational Wellness**: A sense of purpose inspires meaningful contributions in your career.
- **Social Wellness**: Shared spiritual practices or values strengthen bonds with others.
- **Environmental Wellness**: Spaces that reflect your values and preferences create a sense of peace and alignment.

Spiritual Wellness Scenario

Despite the growing success of his e-commerce business, Alex has been feeling disconnected and unmotivated. The long hours, constant problem-solving, and never-ending tasks have left him questioning the purpose behind all his hard work. What once felt like an exciting venture now feels like a treadmill of responsibilities, and Alex struggles to reignite the passion and drive that initially fueled his journey.

Determined to find deeper meaning, Alex begins by reflecting on his core values. He realizes that creativity and making a positive impact on others are at the heart of why he started his business. This insight inspires Alex to create a mentorship program for aspiring entrepreneurs, giving him a way to share his knowledge and support others who are just starting their journeys. Through this initiative, Alex finds a renewed sense of purpose in his work.

Next, Alex starts a gratitude practice, jotting down three things he's thankful for each evening. These might include the loyalty of his customers, the support of his team, and the flexibility his business provides to pursue his dreams. Over time, this daily habit shifts Alex's focus from the challenges he faces to the abundance already present in his life, fostering a more positive mindset.

To stay grounded, Alex incorporates mindfulness into his daily routine. Each morning, he spends five minutes in quiet reflection, setting an intention for the day ahead. This simple practice helps Alex start his day with clarity and a sense of calm, even during the busiest periods of his business.

Seeking deeper connection, Alex joins a local business network focused on sustainable and socially responsible practices. Through these interactions, he finds a supportive community of like-minded entrepreneurs who share his values. The exchange of ideas and encouragement from this group provides Alex with fresh inspiration and a sense of belonging.

Finally, Alex makes time to explore nature, scheduling weekly hikes at a nearby park. These moments of solitude in the natural world help him recharge, reconnect with his goals, and reflect on the bigger picture. The balance he finds in these quiet, reflective moments carries over into his work and personal life, helping him navigate challenges with a greater sense of ease and purpose.

By embracing these practices, Alex rebuilds his sense of purpose and strengthens his spiritual resilience. Without these changes, he risked burnout and losing sight of what truly mattered to him. Instead, Alex now feels more grounded, fulfilled, and ready to face future challenges with confidence, knowing his work aligns with his values and supports his long-term vision.

Spiritual Wellness
Conclusion and Reflection Activity

Spiritual resilience helps you stay grounded and focused on what truly matters, giving you the strength to face life's challenges with clarity and purpose. It's about connecting with your values, finding meaning in your experiences, and cultivating hope—even in difficult times.

Take a moment to reflect on your spiritual habits and ask yourself:

- *What brings me a sense of purpose or meaning?*

- *How can I incorporate a practice, like gratitude or reflection, into my daily life?*

Examples to Get Started:

- If helping others gives you purpose, consider volunteering at a local organization or offering support to someone in need.
- If gratitude resonates with you, start a simple daily practice of writing down one thing you're thankful for each morning.
- If quiet reflection helps you center yourself, set aside 5-10 minutes each day for meditation, prayer, or journaling.

Reflection Activity:

Write down one small step you'll take this week to nurture your sense of purpose or meaning. At the end of the week, reflect on these questions:

- *How did this practice impact my mindset and well-being?*

- *Did it help me feel more connected to my values or purpose?*

- *What's one new step I can take next to continue strengthening my spiritual resilience?*

Always Remember:

Spiritual resilience doesn't just enhance your personal sense of purpose—it ripples out into every area of wellness. By cultivating spiritual resilience, you gain emotional balance, strengthen your social connections, and make more intentional choices that align with your values and goals.

Spiritual resilience isn't about having all the answers, it's about staying connected to what gives your life meaning. Celebrate every small step you take toward a more purposeful, grounded existence. These moments of connection and reflection are the foundation of a resilient and fulfilling life.

Disclaimer: *This section focuses on spiritual resilience as a personal journey of connection, purpose, and meaning. It is not tied to any specific religion or belief system. If you're exploring spiritual questions within a religious framework, consider seeking guidance from your faith community or leaders.*

Environmental Wellness
Understanding
Environmental Wellness and Resilience
(This is about your personal space)

Environmental wellness is about creating a physical space that supports your health, comfort, and well-being. It involves maintaining a clean, organized, and nurturing environment that helps you feel safe and focused. Environmental wellness isn't just about where you live, it's about how your surroundings impact your mental and physical health.

In your daily life, environmental wellness reduces stress and increases productivity. A clutter-free, well-organized space allows you to focus better, relax more deeply, and feel at ease in your environment. Connecting with nature—whether through sunlight, fresh air, or greenery—also enhances your well-being.

Building environmental resilience helps you adapt to changes in your surroundings, whether it's moving to a new home, facing natural disasters, or creating a calming space during stressful times. It empowers you to shape your environment into one that supports your goals and overall wellness.

This chapter will offer practical strategies to enhance environmental wellness and resilience. You'll learn how to declutter, incorporate nature into your space, and create an environment that fosters peace and productivity.

The Core Components of Environmental Resilience

Note: For the purposes of this chapter, "environmental wellness" refers to your personal space—the surroundings you directly control and shape to support your well-being.

1. Safety and Security

Environmental wellness begins with ensuring your personal space feels safe and secure. This involves physical measures, such as locks, alarms, or secure storage, as well as creating an emotionally safe environment where you can relax without fear or stress. Feeling safe is essential to mental well-being and allows you to focus on your goals without distraction. For some, this might mean addressing safety concerns in a shared living situation or taking steps to feel secure when living alone for the first time.

Example: A college student living in an off-campus apartment for the first time installs a door chain and ensures windows are securely locked. They also keep emergency contacts nearby and arrange for regular check-ins with friends or family to create a sense of connection and security.

2. Organization, Decluttering, and Cleaning

An organized and clutter-free environment supports mental clarity, reduces stress, and enhances productivity. By taking steps to organize belongings, eliminate unnecessary items, and keep the space clean, you create a peaceful and functional atmosphere. Cleaning is equally vital—it maintains the health of your space and prevents stress caused by mess or chaos. A tidy environment not only reflects but also reinforces a calm and focused mindset.

Example: A family sets a weekly schedule for cleaning shared spaces, like the kitchen and living room, ensuring the home remains welcoming and functional for everyone. Similarly, professionals organize their workspace by filing away old papers, clearing their desk of unnecessary items, and wiping down surfaces to create a fresh, focused area.

3. Comfort and Functionality

Your personal space should work for you, meeting your specific needs while also being comfortable and inviting. Functionality means designing a space that supports your daily activities, whether that's work, study, or relaxation, while comfort ensures the space feels like a retreat where you can recharge. When your environment is both functional and comfortable, it fosters resilience by helping you handle life's demands with ease.

Example: A factory worker keeps their locker area organized with essentials, such as gloves, snacks, and a water bottle, so they always feel prepared for their shift. At home, they create a cozy living room space with a comfortable chair and good lighting for unwinding after work. Similarly, a student ensures their desk is equipped with ergonomic tools like a supportive chair and proper lighting to balance study sessions with physical comfort.

4. Sensory Balance

The sensory elements of your personal space—lighting, sounds, smells, and even textures—play a significant role in influencing your mood and energy. Achieving sensory balance means adjusting these factors to create a calming or energizing environment depending on your needs. For example, calming scents can reduce anxiety, while natural light can improve focus and boost mood. By curating your sensory environment, you support both mental and emotional wellness.

Example: A student enhances their study space by opening the blinds to let in natural light, playing soft instrumental music to aid focus, and using lavender-scented candles to reduce stress. Similarly, a professional working in a home office uses adjustable lighting, noise-canceling headphones, and pillows to create a space that's both productive and comfortable.

5. Personalization and Ownership

When your space reflects your personality, values, and goals, it fosters a sense of ownership and belonging. Personalizing your environment with meaningful touches—such as photos, plants, or motivational quotes—makes it uniquely yours, creating a stronger connection to your space. A personalized environment inspires positivity and can serve as a source of motivation and comfort during challenging times.

Example: A college student decorates their room with photos of family and friends, a vision board for their goals, and colorful bedding to make the space feel like home. Similarly, a professional adds inspirational quotes and framed achievements to their office, reminding them of their purpose and accomplishments.

Practical Strategies for Polishing Up Environmental Resilience

Environmental resilience is about creating a personal space that supports your well-being, reduces stress, and nurtures your daily life. Whether it's your home, workplace, or digital environment, the way you manage your surroundings can significantly impact your mood, focus, and productivity. By designing a space that feels safe, organized, and restorative, you lay the foundation for a more balanced and resilient life.

Environmental resilience isn't about having the perfect space, it's about making small, intentional changes that work for your unique needs and circumstances.

1. Declutter

An organized space reduces mental clutter and increases focus.

- **Strategy**: Dedicate 10 minutes a day to tidying up one area of your home or workspace.
  Example: A student spends 10 minutes clearing their desk each evening, ensuring a clean and distraction-free space for studying the next day.
- **Why It Works**: Decluttering creates a sense of control and calm, making your environment more supportive and less stressful.

2. Add Nature

Incorporating natural elements fosters a calming and restorative atmosphere.

- **Strategy**: Add plants, use natural light, or include earthy tones and textures in your space.
  Example: An entrepreneur places a small plant on their desk and adjusts their workstation to sit near a window with natural light.
- **Why It Works**: Nature-inspired elements reduce stress, boost creativity, and improve overall well-being.

3. Create Zones

Designating specific areas for work, relaxation, and play helps maintain organization and focus.

- **Strategy**: Divide your space into functional zones to support different activities.
  Example: A parent working from home creates a dedicated workspace at the dining table and sets up a corner for family relaxation with cozy seating and books.
- **Why It Works**: Clear zones minimize distractions and make it easier to switch between tasks and mindsets.

4. Maintain Safety and Security

A secure environment fosters peace of mind and reduces stress.

- **Strategy**: Regularly check and maintain locks, alarms, or other safety features in your home or workspace.
  Example: A college student living alone for the first time installs a smart lock and uses timers to ensure lights are on when they return home at night.
- **Why It Works**: Feeling safe in your space allows you to focus on your goals without unnecessary worry or distraction.

5. Limit Digital Clutter

A clutter-free digital space reduces overwhelm and distractions.

- **Strategy**: Organize your files, clear your inbox, and reduce notifications to streamline your digital environment.
  Example: A professional spends 15 minutes each Friday archiving old emails and organizing project folders for the upcoming week.
- **Why It Works**: Managing digital clutter improves focus, reduces stress, and supports productivity in today's tech-driven world.

Environmental Resilience is about creating a space that promotes balance, well-being, and productivity. However, even with a strong plan, challenges can emerge. These obstacles often fall into two categories: internal struggles, such as procrastination or emotional attachment to clutter, and external barriers, like shared spaces or limited resources. Recognizing and addressing these challenges is key to creating an environment that truly supports your overall wellness.

Obstacles to Building Environmental Wellness

Building environmental wellness involves crafting a space that nurtures your well-being and supports your goals. However, internal and external challenges can make it difficult to maintain a harmonious environment. Identifying these barriers is the first step toward creating a space that fosters resilience, balance, and personal growth.

Internal Obstacles:

Procrastination

Avoiding the effort required to declutter or organize personal spaces can lead to continued stress from a disorganized environment. Tasks pile up, creating a cycle of avoidance and overwhelm.

- **Red Flag:** You find yourself frequently saying, "I'll get to it tomorrow," but the clutter only grows.
- **How to Overcome It:**
    - ➢ Break tasks into smaller steps. For example, focus on one drawer, one shelf, or one corner of a room instead of the entire space.
    - ➢ Set a timer for 10 minutes and commit to tidying or organizing it until the timer ends. Often, starting is the hardest part, and this method lowers the barrier to entry.

> Reward yourself after completing even a small task. Celebrate progress to stay motivated.

Lack of Awareness

Not realizing how much your environment influences well-being can make it difficult to recognize areas that need improvement. Factors like poor lighting, clutter, or digital distractions may go unnoticed but contribute to irritability, stress, or fatigue.

- **Insight Tip:** If you often feel unfocused or irritable, pause to evaluate whether your space may be contributing to those feelings.
- **How to Overcome It:**
    > Spend a week observing your environment and jotting down how different areas make you feel. Do certain spaces cause stress or distraction, while others feel calming or energizing?

    > Research simple environmental wellness practices, such as optimizing natural light, reducing clutter, or introducing plants, and experiment with small, manageable changes.

    > Enlist a trusted friend or family member to offer their perspective on your space. An outside viewpoint may reveal things you overlook.

Emotional Attachment

Holding onto items with sentimental value can prevent you from creating a more functional and peaceful environment. These items may no longer serve a purpose, but the emotional connection makes them difficult to let go of.

- **Mindset Tip:** If you're keeping objects out of guilt rather than joy, it may be time to reevaluate their role in your life.
- **How to Overcome It:**
  - ➤ Use the "joy test" popularized by organizational experts: If an item doesn't spark joy or serve a practical purpose, consider donating or repurposing it.
  - ➤ Take photos of sentimental items before letting them go. This preserves the memory without keeping the physical object.
  - ➤ Set clear boundaries for sentimental items, such as limiting them to a single box or shelf, to ensure they don't overtake your space.

External Obstacles:

Limited Resources

Improving your environment can sometimes feel like an expensive task, especially if you associate wellness with high-end furniture, gadgets, or decor.

- **Quick Fix:** Many effective improvements are cost-free or inexpensive, like decluttering, rearranging furniture, or introducing natural elements.
- **How to Overcome It:**
  - ➤ Focus on what's already available. Rearrange furniture to optimize space, use natural light creatively, or repurpose containers for organization.
  - ➤ Look for budget-friendly solutions like thrifted decor, DIY projects, or online resources for free design ideas.
  - ➤ Incorporate nature into your space by using free or inexpensive items, like branches, stones, or small plants from your local area.

Lack of Time

A busy schedule can make it hard to prioritize organizing and maintaining your environment, leaving it chaotic and stressful.

- **Efficiency Tip:** Even dedicating 5–10 minutes a day to tidying can yield significant results over time.
- **How to Overcome It:**
  - ➤ Incorporate tidying into existing routines. For example, clean your desk before starting

work or tidy the kitchen while waiting for your coffee to brew.

➤ Use scheduling apps or reminders to block out specific times for organizing your space.

➤ Tackle quick, high-impact tasks, like clearing your desk or sorting one drawer, to create a sense of accomplishment.

Shared Spaces

Living or working in shared environments can present unique challenges, especially when others don't share your priorities for cleanliness or organization.

- **Resolution Idea:** Focus on improving your personal areas while encouraging open communication about shared spaces.
- **How to Overcome It:**
  ➤ Use "I" statements to express how the environment impacts your well-being and encourage collaboration. Openly communicate with housemates, coworkers, or family members to establish shared goals for maintaining a supportive space.
  ➤ Create personal sanctuaries. Designate specific personal areas, like a desk or a corner of a room, where you have full control over the environment. Ensure these spaces are organized, calming, and aligned with your wellness goals.
  ➤ Collaborate on shared spaces. Work together to set boundaries and organize shared spaces, such as agreeing on zones for

personal items or cleaning schedules. Encourage collective responsibility by framing organization efforts as a team project that benefits everyone.

A Thought on Environmental Wellness Challenges

Crafting a space that promotes calm, productivity, and balance goes beyond appearance. it's about designing an environment that aligns with your well-being and goals. Challenges like physical clutter, digital distractions, or feelings of insecurity are common, but they don't have to stand in your way. By making small, consistent adjustments and applying practical strategies, you can transform your surroundings into a source of stability and growth.

Reflection Activity: What's Next?

Take a moment to reflect and ask yourself:

- *What's one obstacle I'm ready to tackle?*

- *Which solution feels most realistic to implement this week?*

Write down your plan and commit to trying it.

Even minor improvements can have a significant impact on how you feel and function in your space.

Having explored specific obstacles and their solutions, let's reflect on how cultivating environmental resilience can influence more than just your immediate surroundings. Let's explore the broader impact of environmental resilience and how creating a balanced, nurturing space supports all eight areas of wellness, enhancing your overall well-being.

The Broader Impact of Environmental Resilience on the other Areas of Wellness

Environmental resilience supports your well-being by creating a space that nurtures and sustains you. Its influence includes:

- **Physical Wellness**: A clean, safe environment encourages healthy habits like cooking and exercising.
- **Intellectual Wellness**: A well-designed space supports focus and productivity for learning or work.
- **Emotional Wellness**: Organized and calming spaces reduce stress and promote mental clarity.
- **Financial Wellness**: Managing your space efficiently can reduce waste and save money.
- **Occupational Wellness**: A functional and organized workspace boosts productivity and job satisfaction.
- **Social Wellness**: An inviting environment fosters stronger connections with friends and family.
- **Spiritual Wellness**: Spaces that reflect your values and preferences create a sense of peace and alignment.

Environmental Wellness Scenario

Alex, our dedicated entrepreneur, realizes that his chaotic workspace is taking a toll on his focus, productivity, and overall sense of well-being. Piles of paperwork dominate his desk, constant phone notifications pull him away from tasks, and the noisy surroundings make it difficult to concentrate. Recently, a break-in at a nearby office building has added a layer of anxiety, making Alex feel less secure in his work environment.

Determined to regain control, Alex begins by decluttering his workspace. He dedicates just 10 minutes each morning to organizing his desk and filing important documents. Within a week, Alex notices it's easier to find what he needs, and the visual clutter that once distracted him is gone. The sense of order helps him start each day with a clearer mind.

Next, Alex adds natural elements to his office. He brings in a couple of low maintenance plants and positions his desk near a window to take advantage of natural light. These small but meaningful changes make the space feel more inviting and calming, which helps Alex feel more energized and focused throughout the day.

Recognizing the importance of an efficient layout, Alex reorganizes his workspace into designated zones. His desk becomes a clutter-free area strictly for work, a cozy corner with a comfortable chair is reserved for breaks, and a storage section is used for supplies. This intentional organization streamlines Alex's workflow and reduces the mental fatigue caused by a chaotic environment.

To address his security concerns, Alex invests in smart locks and a basic security camera system for his office. Knowing that his space is better protected gives Alex peace of mind, allowing him to focus on his work without constant worry.

Finally, Alex tackles the digital clutter that had been adding to his stress. He unsubscribes from unnecessary email lists, silences non-essential notifications, and organizes his inbox into categories for quick access. With fewer distractions and a more manageable workload, Alex feels more in control of his time and priorities.

These intentional adjustments not only improve Alex's focus and productivity but also reduce stress and create a sense of harmony in his environment. Without these changes, Alex risked burnout from the overwhelming mental and physical toll of a disorganized and chaotic space. By building environmental resilience, Alex transforms his workspace into a supportive foundation for both personal and professional growth.

Environmental Wellness
Conclusion and Reflection Activity

Your environment shapes your daily life in countless ways. By creating a space that nurtures your well-being, you set the stage for a more balanced and resilient life. A supportive environment can reduce stress, boost productivity, and provide a sense of calm amidst life's challenges.

Take a moment to reflect on your current environment and ask yourself:

- *Does my space support my well-being, or does it add to my stress?*
- *What's one change I can make to improve it, like decluttering, organizing, or adding a personal touch?*
- *Have I ever thought about reducing or deleting junk emails? How could a cleaner inbox improve my daily focus?*

Examples to Get Started:

- If your desk feels chaotic, take 10 minutes to organize it and remove unnecessary clutter.
- If your living space feels impersonal, add a plant, a photo, or a favorite piece of art to make it more welcoming.
- If your inbox is overwhelming, start by unsubscribing from one unnecessary mailing list today and deleting old emails you no longer need.

Reflection Activity:

Choose one area to improve this week. It could be your workspace, a common area, or your inbox. Write down your goal and track your progress. At the end of the week, reflect on these questions:

- *How did this change impact my mood, focus, or stress levels?*
- *Did it make my space feel more supportive and calming?*
- *What's one additional step I can take to build on this progress?*

Always Remember:

When your environment supports your well-being, you feel calmer, more focused, and better able to manage stress. This creates a ripple effect that enhances your emotional resilience, productivity, and overall quality of life. A supportive environment sets the foundation for thriving in all areas of wellness.

Even small changes in your environment can lead to big improvements in your well-being. Celebrate each step you take toward creating a space that truly supports you, it's an investment in your daily happiness and resilience. Remember, your environment is your sanctuary. Make it a place where you can thrive.

Disclaimer: *The strategies in this section are designed to help you build environmental resilience by improving your personal space. However, some challenges, such as housing conditions or financial constraints, may require additional support or resources. If you face significant environmental challenges, consider seeking guidance from community resources or professionals.*

Part 3
A Resilient Life: The Journey Forward

Tying It All Together
Your Path to Resilience

As we reach the final chapters of this book, take a moment to reflect on how resilience is shaping your life. You've explored the eight areas of wellness—Physical, Intellectual, Emotional, Financial, Occupational, Social, Spiritual, and Environmental—each playing a critical role in fostering long-term growth and fulfillment.

To bring this to life, let's revisit Alex's journey—not as a story to follow, but as a reminder of what's possible when small, intentional steps are taken toward resilience.

Alex's Journey to Resilience: A Blueprint for Change

When Alex started, he was a driven entrepreneur, but his dedication to his business came at a cost. Long hours, mounting stress, and neglected self-care left him burned out and questioning his direction. Change didn't happen overnight, but by applying the principles of resilience in each area of wellness, he gradually built a life of balance and purpose.

Here's how resilience played a role in his transformation:

- **Physical Resilience**: Prioritizing sleep, healthy eating, and movement restored his energy. Morning walks became a time for reflection, helping both his body and mind.

- **Intellectual Resilience**: Embracing continuous learning helped him adapt to changes in his industry, revitalizing his business and reinforcing his ability to grow.

- **Emotional Resilience**: Mindfulness and reframing setbacks allowed him to navigate stress with clarity and composure. He built stronger personal and professional relationships as a result.

- **Financial Resilience**: Tracking expenses and setting financial boundaries provided security and peace of mind, reducing stress and allowing for future opportunities.

- **Occupational Resilience**: Setting boundaries, delegating, and aligning his work with long-term goals helped him rediscover passion in his career while maintaining balance.

- **Social Resilience**: Strengthening ties with loved ones and colleagues created a network of support and encouragement, reinforcing his motivation.

- **Spiritual Resilience**: Practicing gratitude and reflecting on personal values helped him stay grounded and connected to his purpose.

- **Environmental Resilience**: Decluttering and optimizing his workspace created an environment that supported focus, creativity, and calm.

Alex's success didn't come from one massive change but rather from consistent, small improvements that built upon each other. His journey serves as a framework, not a prescription—your path will look different, but the process of strengthening resilience across multiple areas remains the same.

Your Journey Forward: The Interconnected Nature of Wellness

As you reflect on your journey, take a moment to recognize how far you've come. Every small step you've taken has contributed to a stronger foundation of resilience.

Resilience isn't about making one dramatic change, it's about intentional, consistent progress. The areas of wellness— Physical, Intellectual, Emotional, Financial, Occupational, Social, Spiritual, and Environmental—are not separate entities; they are deeply connected, shaping your ability to thrive in all aspects of life.

For example, improving your physical wellness through regular exercise and balanced nutrition can enhance emotional resilience by reducing stress and boosting energy. Strengthening social connections provides emotional support, which in turn builds the confidence needed to take on intellectual challenges or advance in your career.

Wellness is not a collection of isolated habits—it's a dynamic system where progress in one area often fuels growth in another. Recognizing these connections allows you to take a holistic approach to resilience, reinforcing long-term success.

Take a moment to reflect:

- *What small changes have you already made?*
- *Which areas of wellness have you strengthened the most?*
- *Where do you still feel imbalanced?*
- *What small step can you take today to reinforce your resilience?*

As you continue forward, keep track of your successes. Whether through journaling, celebrating milestones, or sharing wins with a trusted friend, tracking your progress will reinforce your motivation and resilience.

Resilience is not about perfection, it's about growing, adapting, and taking intentional steps toward the life you want to build.

Resilience as a Lifelong Process

Resilience is not a one-time achievement—it's a skill that evolves over a lifetime. As your life changes, so will your challenges, priorities, and goals. What works for you today may need to shift in the future, and that's completely natural.

Rather than seeing resilience as a finish line, think of it as a practice that grows stronger with each experience. The setbacks and successes you encounter will shape your ability to adapt and move forward with confidence.

Whenever life feels overwhelming or uncertain, return to what you've learned here. The strategies in this book are tools you can lean on whenever you need to realign your focus, refine your approach, or reinforce your resilience.

Take a moment to reflect:

- *Which areas of wellness have you strengthened the most?*

- *Where do you still feel imbalanced?*

- *What small step can you take today to reinforce your resilience?*

Remember that resilience isn't just about perfection, it's about progress. With every intentional step, you are building a stronger foundation for a balanced, fulfilling life.

The Journey Continues: Resilience as an Evolving Practice

Recognizing how far you've come is essential, but your journey isn't over, it's just the beginning. Resilience is a lifelong process that adapts as you grow, face new challenges, and pursue new opportunities.

Setbacks are stepping stones for growth. They provide opportunities to refine your approach, strengthen your mindset, and adjust your course. Rather than seeing obstacles as barriers, use them as guides toward a stronger, more balanced life.

Whenever you feel uncertain, overwhelmed, or off balance, revisit what you've learned here. The strategies in this book are tools you can return to whenever you need to recalibrate and refocus.

As you move forward, remember that resilience isn't about achieving perfection, it's about consistent progress.

Now, let's put these ideas into action. The next section will expand on creating a personalized resilience plan, helping you set clear, meaningful goals that align with the life you want to build.

Integrating Wellness: The Synergy of Resilience in All Areas

Throughout this book, you've explored how resilience strengthens eight interconnected areas of wellness: Physical, Intellectual, Emotional, Financial, Occupational, Social, Spiritual, and Environmental. Each area plays a crucial role in maintaining balance and preventing burnout, but true resilience isn't about improving them in isolation; it's about recognizing how they work together to create lasting stability and fulfillment.

Resilience thrives on synergy. When you strengthen one area, it naturally supports the others, creating a ripple effect that enhances your overall well-being. For example:

- **Improving your Physical Wellness** (exercise, sleep, nutrition) increases energy and mental clarity, which supports **Intellectual Resilience** (focus, learning, problem-solving).

- **Strengthening Emotional Wellness** (self-awareness, stress regulation) improves communication and interpersonal skills, reinforcing **Social Resilience** (relationships, connections, teamwork).

- **Financial Wellness** (budgeting, saving, reducing stress) directly impacts **Occupational Wellness** by creating stability, reducing work anxiety, and allowing for greater career growth.

- **Spiritual Wellness** (values, purpose, gratitude) provides inner motivation and perspective, influencing both **Emotional** and **Social Wellness** by helping you navigate challenges with clarity and deeper connections.

This synergy is what makes resilience a lifelong practice, not a one-time achievement. The more intentional you become in balancing these areas, the more naturally you'll navigate change, adversity, and personal growth.

As you move forward, think beyond isolated improvements and ask yourself:

- *How can I use what I've learned in one area to strengthen another?*

- *Which small adjustments would create the biggest positive ripple effect in my life?*

- *How can I align my daily habits with my long-term vision for resilience and well-being?*

The ability to integrate wellness across multiple areas is the key to sustainable growth. The next section will provide concrete steps to help you take action beyond this book, maintain momentum, and apply resilience in real-world situations.

The Expanding Power of Resilience

Resilience doesn't just transform your personal well-being, it has a profound effect on your relationships, career, and community. When you cultivate resilience, you inspire those around you to do the same.

While all eight areas of wellness contribute to a balanced and fulfilling life, four areas—Financial, Emotional, Social, and Occupational Resilience—most visibly impact relationships, work, and community dynamics. Strengthening resilience in these areas not only enhances your well-being but also influences those around you in meaningful ways.

- **Financial Resilience:** Managing debt, budgeting wisely, and building financial stability reduces stress and creates opportunities for growth. When you demonstrate financial responsibility, it encourages those in your circle—family, friends, and colleagues—to make more mindful financial decisions.

- **Emotional Resilience:** Regulating stress, managing emotions, and maintaining mental clarity strengthens relationships and enhances communication. By modeling emotional resilience, you create healthier interactions and set an example for handling challenges with composure.

- **Social Resilience:** Nurturing supportive relationships and fostering meaningful connections enhances both personal and professional life. A strong support system benefits you and empowers others to cultivate positive relationships and seek mutual growth.

- **Occupational Resilience:** Finding purpose in your work, setting boundaries, and adapting to career challenges fosters fulfillment and balance. Demonstrating resilience in your profession inspires colleagues and employees to develop healthier work habits, pursue meaningful goals, and prevent burnout.

This interconnected growth extends beyond you. Your commitment to resilience sets an example for those around you. When others see your dedication to balance and well-being, they are more likely to take steps toward improving their own lives.

Your Next Steps: Strengthening Resilience Beyond This Book

Now that you have the knowledge and strategies to build resilience, the next step is making it a consistent part of your life. Change doesn't happen overnight, but small, intentional actions create long-term transformation. Here's how to keep moving forward:

1. Set Clear Intentions

Revisit your Personalized Resilience Plan and identify one specific goal you want to focus on first. If you haven't already, write down a SMART goal for each area of wellness and decide where to begin.

Ask yourself:

- *Which area, if strengthened, would have the biggest impact on my overall well-being right now?*

2. Establish Support & Accountability

Resilience grows stronger when reinforced by a support system. Whether it's through friends, mentors, online communities, or an accountability partner, surrounding yourself with encouragement helps maintain progress.

- *Share your goals with someone who will support and challenge you.*

- *Join communities that align with your wellness and personal growth journey.*

- *Follow content, books, or resources that continue to reinforce resilience strategies.*

3. Monitor & Adjust Your Plan

Your needs and circumstances will change, and so should your resilience strategy. Every few weeks, take a self-checkpoint:

- *What's working well?*

- *What challenges have come up?*

- *What adjustments will help me stay on track?*

Resilience is flexible, not rigid. Modify your approach as needed while staying committed to consistent, meaningful growth.

4. Keep Learning & Expanding Your Perspective

Personal growth never ends, and resilience deepens with continuous learning. Consider expanding your knowledge by:

- *Exploring new strategies that complement your resilience journey.*

- *Studying success stories of individuals who have built resilience in inspiring ways.*

- *Engaging in professional or personal development programs to reinforce your progress.*

5. Take Action—Now

The biggest challenge most people face in personal growth is inaction. Reading and reflecting are valuable, but resilience is built through application.

Ask yourself:

- *What's ONE small action I can take today to move forward?*

The key to lasting resilience isn't perfection—it's momentum. Small, consistent actions build long-term habits, shaping a life where resilience becomes second nature.

The Ripple Effect: Leading by Example

Your resilience doesn't just benefit you—it creates a ripple effect that influences your family, friends, and colleagues. Every time you choose to face challenges with strength, prioritize well-being, and take intentional steps toward growth, you encourage others to do the same.

- Your resilience helps build stronger families, workplaces, and communities.

- It fosters a culture of self-awareness, adaptability, and continuous growth.

- It proves that setbacks aren't the end of the road—they're stepping stones for progress.

This process isn't about reaching an endpoint, it's about evolving. As you continue to build resilience, you'll encounter new challenges, opportunities, and lessons. Each time, you'll be better equipped to respond with greater strength and clarity.

If you ever feel uncertain or need to recalibrate, revisit this book. Every strategy you've explored is a tool you can return to—helping you realign with your goals and continue moving forward.

Each step forward strengthens not only your own resilience but also the collective resilience of those around you.

Continuing Your Growth

If you ever feel uncertain or need to recalibrate, revisit this book. Every strategy you've explored is a tool you can return to—helping you realign with your goals and continue moving forward.

Each step forward strengthens not only your own resilience but also the collective resilience of those around you.

The process doesn't end here, it grows with every challenge and opportunity you face.

Celebrate the Journey

Congratulations! Reaching this point means you've committed to growth, reflection, and action. Whether you've already started making changes or are still mapping out your path, the fact that you've engaged in this process is something to celebrate.

Take a deep breath and acknowledge your progress:

- *What's one small win you can recognize today?*

- *How has progress in one area of wellness positively impacted others?*

Your journey has been about more than just setting goals, it's been about developing a mindset that allows you to adapt, grow, and thrive.

Tracking Your Success

Resilience is strengthened by recognizing and reinforcing progress. Here are a few ways to stay on track:

Reflection Activity:

  o *What strategies have helped you the most?*

  o *How have challenges shaped your growth?*

- **Practical Tools:** Use a journal, habit tracker, or vision board to visualize your progress.

- **Share Your Success:** Discuss your journey with a mentor, accountability partner, or supportive community.

Every step you take strengthens your resilience, helping you build a life that is balanced, fulfilling, and aligned with your values.

Your Personalized Resilience Plan
Putting Your Resilience into Action

Building resilience is not just about understanding the concepts—it's about applying them to your daily life. Your Personalized Resilience Plan will help you turn ideas into action, ensuring that you make meaningful progress in each area of wellness. By setting clear, structured goals, you'll create lasting change that keeps you grounded, focused, and adaptable in the face of challenges.

A strong plan provides clarity, motivation, and measurable steps toward progress. Instead of feeling overwhelmed by everything you'd like to improve, you'll focus on small, intentional steps that build long-term resilience.

Reflection Activity: Identifying Your Focus Areas

Take a few moments to reflect on where you are right now.

- *Which area of wellness feels most in need of attention?*

- *Which area, if improved, would have the greatest positive impact on your overall well-being?*

- *Where in your life do you feel the most stress or imbalance?*

- *Which area do you often neglect or push aside?*

- *What small, positive change could make a noticeable difference in your daily routine?*

Once you've identified the areas where you'd like to grow, the next step is setting goals that are both meaningful and achievable. Using the SMART method (Specific, Measurable, Achievable, Relevant, and Time-bound), you can create a clear path forward, ensuring that your goals align with your long-term vision for resilience and wellness.

Preventing Burnout & Strengthening Resilience with SMART Goals

Resilience isn't just about endurance—it's about strategically adapting and growing in ways that protect your well-being while keeping you on track toward a fulfilling life. To truly integrate resilience into your daily routine and prevent burnout, it's essential to set clear, actionable goals that create meaningful progress.

The SMART framework helps break big, overwhelming challenges into manageable, measurable steps, ensuring that resilience-building becomes a habit rather than an abstract concept.

How SMART Goals Help You Prevent Burnout & Strengthen Resilience

Burnout often stems from mental exhaustion, lack of direction, and feeling stuck. Resilience is the opposite—it's the ability to bounce back, refocus, and move forward with confidence.

SMART goals provide structure in a way that directly counters burnout triggers:

- They prevent overwhelm by turning long-term growth into small, realistic steps.

- They increase motivation by offering clear benchmarks for success.

- They reinforce self-awareness, a key pillar of the Wheel of Success, ensuring that your goals align with your values and energy levels.

- They build momentum, reducing stress and making resilience an ongoing process rather than something you scramble to develop when things get tough.

By setting SMART goals across all eight areas of wellness, you create a balanced approach that strengthens your entire foundation for well-being.

Understanding SMART Goals: The Breakdown

SMART stands for:

- **Specific:** Clearly define what you want to achieve. Avoid vague goals like "I want to be healthier" and instead make it precise, such as "I will walk 30 minutes five times a week."

- **Measurable:** Track your progress with quantifiable metrics. Instead of "I want to read more," try "I will read 10 pages of a book every night before bed."

- **Achievable:** Set realistic goals that challenge you but remain attainable based on your current lifestyle and resources. If you're new to meditation, rather than "I'll meditate for an hour daily," start with "I will practice mindful breathing for 5 minutes each morning."

- **Relevant:** Align your goal with your bigger vision. Ask yourself: "How does this contribute to my resilience and well-being?" If financial stability is your focus, setting a fitness goal might not be the immediate priority— instead, budgeting habits might be more relevant.

- **Time-bound:** Set a clear timeframe. Deadlines create accountability. Instead of "I'll start saving money soon," commit to "I will save $50 per week for the next three months."

Building Resilience with SMART Goals in All 8 Areas of Wellness

To fully integrate resilience into your life, set one SMART goal for each area of wellness using the guidelines above.

- **Physical Wellness** – Building Energy & Preventing Burnout
  SMART Goal Example: "I will go for a brisk 30-minute walk five days a week and track my progress using a fitness app."

- **Intellectual Wellness** – Strengthening Mental Agility & Avoiding Stagnation
  SMART Goal Example: "I will read one book per month related to personal growth or my field of work, starting with 10 pages per day."

- **Emotional Wellness** – Regulating Stress & Enhancing Emotional Stability
  SMART Goal Example: "I will practice mindfulness for 5 minutes every morning for the next 30 days, increasing to 10 minutes by the end of the second month."

- **Financial Wellness** – Reducing Financial Stress & Creating Stability
  SMART Goal Example: "I will save $50 per week by cutting back on non-essential expenses and automate transfers to my savings account for accountability."

- **Occupational Wellness** – Preventing Work Burnout & Finding Purpose
  SMART Goal Example: "I will schedule at least one uninterrupted hour each week to work on career development, such as networking or skill-building."

- **Social Wellness** – Strengthening Relationships & Building Support Systems
  SMART Goal Example: "I will reach out to one friend or family member per week to check in and nurture my connections."

- **Spiritual Wellness** – Aligning Actions with Purpose & Values
  SMART Goal Example: "I will practice gratitude by writing down three things I'm thankful for every evening for the next 60 days."

- **Environmental Wellness** – Creating a Supportive Space for Mental & Physical Well-Being
  SMART Goal Example: "I will declutter one area of my home each weekend, starting with my workspace, to create a stress-free environment."

Making Your Resilience Plan Work for You

Now it's your turn. Take the next step in building resilience by creating SMART goals that support each of the eight areas of wellness. By setting structured, intentional goals, you'll make steady progress toward a more balanced and fulfilling life.

Step 1: Reflect on Your Wellness Areas

Before setting goals, take a moment to assess where you currently stand in each area:

1. Physical Wellness

2. Intellectual Wellness

3. Emotional Wellness

4. Financial Wellness

5. Occupational Wellness

6. Social Wellness

7. Spiritual Wellness

8. Environmental Wellness

Ask yourself and write out your answers:

- *Which areas of feel strong?*

- *Which need the most attention?*

- *Which, if improved, would create the biggest positive impact on my overall well-being?*

Step 2: Set Your SMART Goals

Using the SMART framework (Specific, Measurable, Achievable, Relevant, Time-bound), write one goal for each of the eight areas of wellness.

- **Identify one area of wellness where you want to focus first.** Start here and build momentum.
- **Write SMART goals for the remaining areas**, ensuring they are realistic and meaningful to you.
- **Track your progress** using a journal, habit tracker, or check-ins with a mentor or friend.
- **Celebrate small wins each week** to reinforce motivation and resilience.
- **Adjust goals as needed.** This is about progress, not perfection.

Step 3: Build a Weekly Reflection Habit

To stay on track, set aside time each week to review your progress. Ask yourself:

- *What worked well?*
- *What challenges did I face?*
- *How have small wins in one area impacted other areas of wellness?*
- *What adjustments can I make moving forward?*

Tracking your progress keeps you accountable and motivated. Each small step strengthens your foundation for resilience, helping you stay adaptable, focused, and prepared for whatever life brings.

Your Commitment to Lasting Resilience

Resilience isn't a one-time achievement; it's an evolving process. As you integrate these SMART goals into your life, you'll naturally build momentum toward long-term balance and well-being.

Whenever life throws new challenges your way, revisit this plan. Adjust it. Improve it. Use it as a tool to ensure you continue building a life that strengthens—not drains—you.

The next section will guide you through how to maintain resilience as a lifelong practice and ensure you stay on track even when setbacks arise.

Your journey continues—let's make it stronger, one intentional step at a time.

Resources to Support Your Growth

Your resilience journey continues beyond these pages. If you're looking for further guidance, strategies, and community support, explore these additional resources:

- **Visit Unfryd.com** – Access online courses, downloadable guides, and personalized tools designed to help you integrate resilience into daily life.

- **Subscribe to @AvoidBurnout** on YouTube – Get practical tips, guided exercises, and real-world strategies for strengthening resilience across all areas of wellness.

- **Join our Facebook group, Break Free from Burnout** – Connect with others who are also committed to growth, accountability, and long-term resilience. Engage in discussions, share progress, and find encouragement from like-minded individuals.

These resources aren't extra tasks, they're free tools designed to support you exactly where you are in your journey.

Your Resilient Life Starts Now

Resilience isn't about never falling, it's about having the strength to rise, again and again, no matter what the challenge. Every step forward is proof of your ability to adapt, grow, and persevere.

Each decision you make—to keep going, to keep learning, to keep pushing forward, builds the foundation for a life of balance, fulfillment, and purpose.

Every time you apply the principles of the Wheel of Success—strengthening resilience in each area of wellness—you reinforce your ability to thrive. This isn't just about avoiding burnout; it's about designing a life that energizes and sustains you. Resilience is a lifelong skill, and you now have the tools to master it.

You already have the strength within you to navigate life's challenges, embrace new opportunities, and shape the future you deserve. Trust yourself. Resilience isn't just about overcoming obstacles; it's about actively designing the life you want.

This journey doesn't end here. With every choice you make, you are writing your own story—one of strength, purpose, and lasting growth.

Whether it's a shift in mindset, a new daily habit, or a commitment to self-care, each intentional action strengthens your foundation.

Every time you choose resilience; you reinforce your ability to thrive. You have the knowledge, the power, and the determination to create a life that reflects your values and aspirations.

This is your moment—embrace it, own it, and step forward into your most resilient and fulfilling chapter yet.

Whenever life throws new challenges your way, know that you already have the tools to navigate them.

Resilience is always within reach. Use it, trust it, and keep moving forward.

Your Next Step: Turning Resilience into Action

You've come this far, which means you're ready. But reading alone won't create change—action will.

Right now, take one small step toward resilience.

Ask yourself:

- *What's one area of wellness I can focus on first?*

- *What's one small action I can take today?*

Write it down. Say it out loud. Then go do it.

Because resilience isn't something you hope for, it's something you build. And it starts now.

But remember, resilience isn't a destination; it's a way of living.

Every time you choose growth over fear, progress over perfection, and action over hesitation, you strengthen the foundation of your most resilient life.

This isn't the end of your journey; it's just the beginning.

You already have everything you need to create balance, clarity, and purpose.

Now, let's make sure resilience isn't just something you read about; it's something you live.

- **Make a choice today:** Pick one area of wellness and take a small, intentional action toward strengthening it.

- **Revisit this book as a tool:** Each strategy, reflection, and example is here for you when you need it.

- **Stay accountable:** Find a way to track your progress and connect with others on a similar journey.

Resilience isn't about never facing difficulties; it's about knowing you have the strength to rise every time you do. You've equipped yourself with the knowledge—now it's time to apply it.

This is your moment. Your next step starts today.

Let's build a life of strength, balance, and resilience—one intentional action at a time.

Acknowledgements

I would like to acknowledge my good friend and co-author/contributor on chapters Physical, Intellectual, and Emotional chapters, Troy Heiner, for his fortitude and invaluable input and 'Troyisms' in shaping parts of this book. His quick wit and shared passion for inspiring others to reach higher levels of success have made this journey an amazing experience. (Besides, we share the same birthday and tend to think alike—what are the odds?)

A special thanks to Matt DiMaio, a great mentor and friend, who introduced me to the cutting-edge and truly phenomenal learning platform, The Great Discovery. Your guidance, mentorship and friendship has been invaluable and will never be forgotten!

To all my former students—you know who you are! Listening to and learning from your challenges and triumphs have been the inspiration behind the Wheel of Success, this book, and those to come. Your journeys have shaped this work more than you could ever imagine.

Most especially my wife, for putting up with my long writing and editing sessions in making this happen!

www.ingramcontent.com/pod-product-compliance
Lightning Source LLC
LaVergne TN
LVHW051403080426
835508LV00022B/2947